P9-DHL-456

Top 25-sight locator
map (continues on
inside back cover)

←

Fodor's CITYPACK
venice

by Tim Jepson

Fodor's Travel Publications
New York • Toronto •
London • Sydney • Auckland
www.fodors.com

About This Book

ORGANIZATION

Citypack Venice is divided into six sections to cover the six most important aspects of your visit to Venice. It includes:

- Planning Ahead, Getting There
- Living Venice—Venice Now, Venice Then, Time to Shop, Out and About, Walks, Venice by Night
- Venice's Top 25 Sights
- Venice's Best—best of the rest
- Where to—detailed listings of restaurants, hotels, stores, and nightlife
- Travel facts—packed with practical information

In addition, easy-to-read side panels provide extra facts and snippets, highlights of places to visit and invaluable practical advice.

MAPS

The fold-out map in the wallet at the back of the book is a comprehensive street plan of Venice. The first (or only) grid reference given for each attraction refers to this map. **The Top 25 locator maps** found on the inside front and back covers of the book itself are for quick reference. They show the Top 25 Sights, described on pages 26–50, which are clearly plotted by number (**1**–**25**, not page number) across the city. The second map reference given for the Top 25 sights refers to this map.

ADMISSION CHARGES

For attractions we categorize the standard adult rate as follows:
✋ Expensive (over 5 euros; L10,000), Moderate (3–5 euros; L6–10,000), and Inexpensive (under 3 euros; L6,000).

Contents

Planning Ahead

WHEN TO GO

Avoid July and August, the hottest and busiest months, and plan a visit for April, May, June, September, or October. Hotels are busy from Easter to October, in February during Carnevale, and over Christmas and New Year. Despite the weather, winter can still be a delightful time to see the city.

TIME

Italy is six hours ahead of New York, nine hours ahead of Los Angeles, and one hour ahead of GMT in winter.

AVERAGE DAILY TEMPERATURES

JAN	FEB	MAR	APR	MAY	JUN	JUL	AUG	SEP	OCT	NOV	DEC
43°F	46°F	54°F	59°F	68°F	73°F	79°F	77°F	70°F	61°F	54°F	45°F

Spring (March to May) has a mixture of sunshine and showers, the chill easterly wind, the *bora*, can lower temperatures. Fog occurs occasionally.

Summer (June to August) can be unpredictable; clear skies and searing heat one day followed by sultry grayness and thunderstorms the next.

Fall (September to November) becomes wetter as the season progresses and fog can envelope the city. Again, the *bora* will create a noticeable wind chill.

Winter (December to February) is generally mild but flooding, *acqua alta*, can occur.

WHAT'S ON

February *Carnevale* (Carnival): Pageants, masks, and costumes.

March *Su e zo per i ponti:* A long street race in which competitors run "up and down the bridges" of Venice (second Sunday in month).

April *Festa di San Marco:* A gondola race from Sant'Elena to the Punta della Dogana marks the feast day of Venice's patron saint. Men traditionally give women a red rose.

May *La Sensa:* Venice's mayor re-enacts the Marriage to the Sea, in which the doge would cast a ring into the sea to symbolize the "wedding" of the city to the sea (Sunday after Ascension Day). *Vogalonga:* Literally the "long row," a 20-mile race from Piazza San Marco to Burano and back (Sunday following La Sensa).

June *Biennale:* Venice's international art exhibition takes place every odd-numbered year (Jun–Sep).

July *Festa del Redentore:* Pontoons are laid across the Giudecca canal to the Redentore to celebrate Venice's deliverance from the plague of 1576. People picnic in boats and watch fireworks (third Sunday of the month).

September *Venice Film Festival:* Held on the Lido (early Sep). *Regata Storica:* Historical costume pageant and procession of boats on the Canal Grande, followed by a race between gondoliers (first Sunday of the month).

November *Festa della Salute:* A pontoon is built across the Canal Grande, to the Salute, to celebrate the passing of a plague in 1630 (Nov 21).

VENICE ONLINE

www.enit.it
The main Italian Tourist Board website carries a wealth of information on everything you need to know about the whole country, with Venice getting plenty of attention. There are sections on history, culture, events, activities, accommodations, gastronomy, and plenty of practical tips—available in several languages.

www.emmeti.it
Another Italy-based site, in English and Italian, with a good range of information on Venice and links to other sites. It's strong on local events and offers an online hotel reservation service.

www.turismovenezia.it
This excellent site, in English and Italian, gives a wealth of information via its efficient search engine on every aspect of the city. You'll find details of accommodations, restaurants, and shopping as well as the full lowdown of what to see and do. There's a frequently updated newsletter and good links to other sites.

www.comune.venezia.it
Although aimed as much at local residents as visitors, the Venetian city council's site provides good up-to-date information on cultural activities and historic sites in the city. Look here for the latest on erratically opening museums, city services, and what's on when.

www.virtualvenice.net
A nice, lively site run from Italy with English text, giving plenty of information on everything Venice has to offer. Very good for shopping, accommodations, and lists of restaurants and bars away from the mainstream.

www.initaly.com
This wonderfully enthusiastic site is run by passionate lovers of Italy from the U.S. It's packed with information and articles about the whole country, with quirky tips and insider stories, and makes excellent browsing at the planning stage.

PRIME TRAVEL SITES

www.actv.it
Venice's city transportation system runs this informative site where you'll find full route details, timetables, and fare structures for the vaporetto network—there's even a game involving navigating the Grand Canal.

www.fs-on-line.it
The official site of the Italian State Railways with excellent train information and an easy-to-use search facilty—good for forward planning.

www.promhotels.it
Useful online booking site for hotels in Venice and other Italian destinations, with a large range of accommodations at all prices.

www.fodors.com
A travel-planning site where you can research prices and weather, book tickets, cars, and rooms, and ask fellow travelers questions; links to other sites.

Getting There

BEFORE YOU GO

All visitors to Italy require a valid passport. Visas are not required for US, UK, New Zealand, Canadian, Irish, and Australian citizens, or other EU nationals staying fewer than three months.

Check your insurance coverage and buy a supplementary policy as needed.

MONEY

The euro is the official currency of Italy. Banknotes in denominations of 5, 10, 20, 50, 100, 200 and 500 euros, and coins in denominations of 1, 2, 5, 10, 20, 50 cents and 1 and 2 euros were introduced on 1 January 2002.

50 euros

200 euros

500 euros

ARRIVING

There are direct flights to Venice from all over the world. Venice has two main airports, Marco Polo and Treviso.

40 MILES

Treviso Airport ✈
19 miles to city center
Bus 1hr, 4 euros;
L8,000

Marco Polo Airport ✈
5 miles to city center
Bus 20 minutes, 2.50
euros; L5,000

FROM MARCO POLO

Scheduled internal and international flights (plus a few charters) arrive at Venice's Marco Polo Airport, 5 miles north of the city center. For flight information ☎ 041 260 9260/6111 or recorded information around the clock ☎ 041 238 1590. Connections from Marco Polo to Piazzale Roma take 20–40 minutes and can be made by taxi, blue ATVO buses, or ACTV No. 5 orange city buses. Buy tickets for buses before boarding from the office inside the arrivals terminal. Buses leave from the concourse outside the terminal. Water taxis run to most points within the city (20 minutes), but the prices are high (over 77 euros; L150,000). A less expensive Alilaguna public water launch makes the trip (50 minutes) to San Marco, the Lido, and Zattere. The ticket office is close to the arrivals terminal exit; the dock is immediately outside.

FROM TREVISO

Tiny Treviso airport, 19 miles outside the city, is served mainly by charter flights. A shuttle bus runs to the center of Treviso, from there you can get regular bus and train connections to Venice.

ARRIVING BY TRAIN

Trains to Venice arrive at the Venezia Santa Lucia station, often abbreviated as Venezia SL (☎ 041 715555). The station is at the head of the Grand Canal, five minutes' walk from Piazzale Roma; from the quays outside there are frequent *vaporetto* (1, 82, and others) and *motoscafo* (52) boat services to the rest of the city. Be sure the boat you board is heading in the right direction. Note that many through trains stop on the mainland at Mestre station, confusingly called Venezia Mestre (Venezia M), without continuing to Venice proper. Check your train is destined for Santa Lucia; if it is not, catch one of the frequent connecting services at Mestre for the 15-minute trip across the causeway.

ARRIVING BY CAR

Cars must be left at one of the multi-story parking lots at the Tronchetto (linked by boat 82 to the rest of the city) or the more central Piazzale Roma, from where you can walk or catch boats 1, 41, 42, 51, 52, 61, 62, 71, 72, 82. Rates start at about 8 euros; L15, 000 a day. There are no free parking lots and no other parking places; cars parked elsewhere will be towed away and in summer, lines on the causeway approaching the city are common. Consider leaving your car in Mestre and then taking a train.

GETTING AROUND

Venice is compact and the occasions when you need public transportation are suprisingly few. But while walking in such a beautiful place is an obvious pleasure, so too, is the experience of taking a boat (► 89). Venice's public transportation is run by the Azienda del Consorzio Trasporti Veneziano (ACTV), which comprises the *vaporetti* ferry service in the city and around the lagoon, as well as buses connecting Venice with mainland areas. You can obtain tickets and pick up timetables and route maps from the ACTV information office in Piazzale Roma (☎ 041 522 2633).

For more detailed information about public transportation ► 89–90.

HANDY HINT

Four tourist tickets are available on ACTV boats: the *Biglietto 24 Ore*, valid for 24 hours; the *Biglietto 72 Ore*, valid for three days; the *Biglietto Itinerario*, valid for travel on Line 12 to Murano, Burano, and Torcello for 12 hours; and a 7-day ticket, also valid for the islands as well as ACTV buses to the airport.

VISITORS WITH DISABILITIES

Venice is difficult for visitors with disabilities. Streets are narrow, there are numerous bridges, and moving on and off boats is almost impossible. Hotels, galleries, and other public spaces are often in historic buildings where conservation restrictions limit access. This said, matters are improving, and the Venetian and Italian state tourist offices can provide lists of appropriate hotels and contact details for Italian associations for those with disabilities.

Living
Venice

Venice Now

Above: *the colossal church of San Nicolò da Tolentini, popular for weddings*
Right: *boats moored on the Grand Canal*

Venice has been seducing visitors for centuries, its impossible watery setting and fairy-tale appearance casting a spell whose potency remains undimmed by mass tourism. One of the city's greatest charms, of course, is how little it has changed over the years, the views painted by Giovanni Bellini, Canaletto, and others hundreds of years ago are more or less the views you see today. Yet while historic Venice and contemporary Venice are virtually the same —at least to look at—the city also belongs to the 21st century.

Venice sits at the heart of a lagoon, separated from the open sea by a line of defensive sand bars. Its 118 islands, over 400 bridges, 3000 alleys, and 170 canals are divided into six districts, or *sestieri*. Three lie west of the Grand Canal, the watery highway that bisects the city (San Polo, Dorsoduro, and Santa Croce) and three to the east (San Marco, Castello, and

Above: *the island of Burano attracts visitors with its striking facades*
Left: *traveling by gondola*

A WAY WITH WORDS

• Venice has a variety of unusual words to describe parts of the city. A *campo* (literally "field") is a square but only one square in the city is worthy of the word "piazza"–Piazza San Marco. A small square is a *campiello* or *campazzo*. *Calle* is the name for a street, *riva* or *fondamenta* the name for a street running along a canal; *ruga* is the term for an important street or one lined with stores; a *ramo* ("branch") is a short street or the extension of a street with the same name and a *salizzada* is a paved street. A *piscina* is a pool or turning basin for boats and a *rio terra* a canal that has been filled in to become a street.

BEST MOMENTS

• These are often away from the main sights. So take a boat along the Grand Canal just for the ride, or see the Rialto markets at the crack of dawn before the crowds arrive. Little beats an aerial view, preferably from the top of San Giorgio Maggiore, and no city offers more to those who wander at random.

SPECIAL TICKETS

• Keen sightseers should take advantage of Venice's combined ticket offers. The first, valid indefinitely, gives entry to the municipal museums and includes the Doge's Palace, the Museo Correr, the Palazzo Mocenigo, the Museo dell'Arte Vetrario on Murano, and the Scuola dei Merletti on Burano. Most of the city's famous churches now charge a small admission fee; some have combined forces and offer a 3-day ticket entry to six landmark churches including the Madonna dell'Orto and Santo Stefano.

Cannaregio). The city may look labyrinthine, but the web of streets is easier to navigate than it first appears. Distances are short, and a few key streets wend through the maze. The Rialto, Venice's old commercial heart, and Piazza San Marco, the city's most famous square, provide central points of reference.

Once you have grasped the city's layout, the best way to see it is one area at a time. Study the map to sort out the top 25 sights, and which more minor sights lie close to each other. Only three bridges cross the Grand Canal, so plan itineraries carefully to avoid unnecessary walking. Also learn to use the little ferry services, or *traghetti*, which cross the Canal at strategic points. And do not overlook the *vaporetti*, or water buses, as a means of sight-seeing, particularly the No. 1, which lumbers up and down the Grand Canal.

In a city where every turn reveals a lovely view or evocative corner, choosing what to see if time is short can be difficult. This said, on your first morning see anything in Venice except Piazza San Marco, the Doge's Palace, or the Basilica di

Far left: *pastel-colored houses line the backstreets of Burano*
Left: *early morning at the fish market*
Above: Regata Storico

San Marco. Start instead with something more modest, perhaps a cappuccino in a sleepy *campo*, or something whose crowds don't turn you against the city at the first acquaintance.

Once you have a feel for the city's more intimate side, move to the bigger draws; to the two key galleries, the Accademia and Collezione Peggy Guggenheim; to the two major churches, SS Giovanni e Paolo and Santa Maria Gloriosa

FATAL STEP

• Venice's civilian casualties during the two world wars of the 20th century numbered around 200, most of whom, it is claimed, walked into canals during the black-out and were drowned.

GONDOLAS

• Back in the 18th century there were around 14,000 gondolas plying the canals. Today there are only around 400 still in use, all remarkably uniform. They measure about 36 feet long and 4 feet wide. The right-hand side is slightly longer than the left—the resulting lean and asymmetry counters the weight of the gondolier. Each weighs about 700kg and has 280 separate components. Eight types of wood are used in their construction: elm, oak, fir, lime, larch, walnut, cherry, and mahogany—and according to 16th-century law, are all painted with seven layers of black lacquer. A ninth wood, beech, is used for the oar. The walnut oar-rest, or *forcola*, is oiled and carved to suit individual gondoliers, and allows the oar to be used in at least eight different positions. Propelled by a single oarsman standing at the back of the boat, these elegant shallow-draft vessels are the ideal shape and depth for penetrating even the narrowest and shallowest canals.

Above: *mooring poles add color to the murky water*
Right: *a stone hand sculpture stands on the waterside promenade known as the Riva degli Schiavoni*
Far right: *the wedding-cake facade of the Chiesa dei Scalzi*

ACQUA ALTA

• Visit Venice between November and April and you run the risk of encountering *acqua alta* or "high water," when winter weather, winds, and high tides combine to submerge large areas. Raised wooden walkways, *passarelle*, are laid out on key routes to help people get around.

dei Frari; to the two best museums, the Correr and Ca' d'Oro; and the finest *scuole*, the Scuola Grande di San Rocco and Scuola Grande di San Giorgio degli Schiavoni. Thereafter decide between more museums—perhaps the Ca' Rezzonico and Museo Storico Navale—or smaller churches—Madonna dell'Orto, San Giovanni in Bragora, or Santa Maria dei Miracoli. Finally brace yourself for the big two: the Palazzo Ducale (Doge's Palace) and Basilica di San Marco (St. Mark's).

But in seeing the sights do not fall into the all-too-easy assumption that Venice is a dead city sustained by and for visitors. Venice is a contemporary city facing a series of contemporary problems. As you explore bear in mind that this magical place is also one where people live, work, and bring up their families in what, on an everyday level, must be one of the most inconvenient towns in the world. Added to that, Venice faces immense problems caused by

flooding and industrial pollution. It may have stopped sinking, but dredging, land reclamation, and global warming are taking their toll. All of these problems have exacerbated the danger of flooding during high tides. The proposed system of steel dykes (known as MOSE) designed to close the lagoon entrances during danger periods is highly controversial, with most conservationists—who feel the lagoon's ecosystem will be irreparably damaged—opposed to the scheme.

Plans to resolve these problems advance at snail's pace and many Venetians have given up the struggle and expense of city-center life to move to the big industrial towns of Mestre or Marghera on the edge of the lagoon. The population has plummeted since 1940 from 160,000 to around 65,000. But Venice's fleeing natives have remained Venetian at heart, commuting by boat to work, quick to absolve their beloved city from the perceived sins of the city fathers. Whatever the future holds, Venetians will remain passionately proud of their city, and millions of tourists will remember its beauty for the rest of their lives.

VITAL STATISTICS

● It is estimated that there are 3,000 alleys in Venice. Laid end to end they would stretch for 120 miles.

● Although Venice has an estimated 400 bridges, only one has more than a single arch, the Ponte dei tre Archi (Bridge of the Three Arches), close to the San Giobbe.

● The city has around 450 souvenir stores. Fifty percent of the local workforce is involved in tourism. In contrast, Venice has under 20 plumbers.

15

Venice Then

MARCO POLO

Born in Venice in 1254, Marco Polo left with his father in 1269 on a journey that would last two decades. In 1275 he arrived in the court of Kublai Khan, where he served the Mongol emperor until 1295. In 1298 he was captured by the Genoese. It was from prison that he dictated his *Description of the World*.

ANTONIO VIVALDI

Vivaldi was born in Venice in 1678. Although ordained as a priest, he devoted his life to music, teaching violin at La Pieta orphanage, whose girls received music training as part of their state-funded education. La Pieta's orchestra enabled Vivaldi to create a wealth of music compositions, including the famous "Four Seasons."

800 BC Sporadic settlement of the lagoon by the Venetii and Euganei tribes.

250 BC Rome conquers *Venetia* and founds important colonies at Padua, Verona, Altinium, and Aquileia.

AD 402 Alaric the Goth sacks Altinium and other northeastern colonies. A vision of the Virgin guides refugees to an island in the lagoon.

421 According to legend Venice is founded on March 25, the Feast Day of the Virgin Mary.

453 Aquileia is sacked by Attila the Hun, prompting another exodus of refugees to the lagoon.

697 The first Doge (leader) of Venice, Paoluccio Anafesto, is elected.

810 Lagoon dwellers gather on the more easily defended islands of the Rialto.

828 Venetian merchants steal the relics of St. Mark from Alexandria.

1171 Venice's six districts, *sestieri*, are founded.

1204 Venice sacks Constantinople and acquires much of the former Byzantine Empire.

From left to right: *Marco Polo saying goodbye to his family, 1271;*
Bellini's oil painting (1496) of a procession in St. Mark's Square;
the Campanile in Piazza San Marco collapses in 1902;
Venice under water during the floods of 1966

1380 Victory over the Genoese at the Battle of Chioggia. Venice wins naval supremacy in the Adriatic and Mediterranean.

1406 Venice defeats Padua and Verona to lay the foundations of a mainland empire.

1453 Venice's power is at its height, but the Turks take Constantinople. Over the next 200 years they will also take Cyprus and Crete.

1498 Vasco da Gama's discovery of the Cape route to the East weakens Venice's trading monopolies.

1718 The loss of Morea marks the end of Venice's maritime empire.

1797 Napolean invades Italy: the last doge abdicates and the Venetian Republic comes to an end.

1814 After Napolean's defeat, the Congress of Vienna cedes Venice and the Veneto to Austria.

1866 Venice joins a united Italy.

1966 Devastating floods ravage Venice.

1988 Work on MOSE flood barrier begins, it remains unfinished.

COURTESANS AND VENETIAN GREED

At the end of the 16th century, the city contained 11,654 women of the night. This compared with 2,889 patrician women; 1,936 burghers; and 2,508 nuns. Taxes from prostitution funded an estimated 12 galleys. In the 18th century, according to one contemporary report, "Venetians did not taste their pleasures, but swallowed them whole." Another observer reported that "the men are women, the women are men, and all are monkeys."

17

Time to Shop

BURANO LACE

Although lace was made by women of all classes during the Middle Ages, it was the development of an intricate stitch known as Burano point that made the eponymous island (➤ 21) famous for its lace. Mass production in the 19th century devastated the industry, and today only a handful of women make lace by hand. Much of what you see for sale in Burano and the rest of Venice is foreign or machine-made. If you want the real thing, visit stores such as Jesurum, and be prepared to pay (➤ 80).

Venice was one of the world's greatest trading centers for 500 years before its decline in the 17th and 18th centuries. Sumptuous goods from all corners of the globe filled its markets, stores, and warehouses. Today, its trade is less exotic and wide-reaching.

You will still find many designer names and great Italian fashion, accessories, shoes, and other leatherware. But this is not a city to compare with other Italian centers such as Rome, Milan, or Florence. Space in the city is at a premium, so choice is relatively limited, and transportation costs mean prices in stores are often higher than elsewhere.

This said, Venice's extraordinary history has bequeathed the city several unique shopping possibilities. The artisan traditions of Murano and Burano, for example, make glass and lace from these two lagoon islands good buys— though you need to be on your guard against inferior, foreign-produced products. Glass trinkets can also provide some of Venice's most kitsch souvenirs.

Far left/left: *the windows of major fashion chains will catch the eye with displays of the latest designs from Milan, but smaller, interesting shops will delight as well*
Above: *a glass-making workshop on the island of Murano*

With the revival of the Venice carnival over the last few years stores selling and producing the traditional masks (*maschere*) worn by revelers have proliferated. Some masks are mass-produced—but often still beautiful—while others are painstakingly created by hand in workshops (➤ 80–81) around the city.

Marbled paper, another traditional Venetian craft, has also enjoyed a revival and since the 1970s stores across the city sell paper products. The craft is almost a thousand years old, and spread from Japan to Persia and the Arab world during the Middle Ages. It reached Europe in about the 15th century. Mass-produced papers are perfectly good, but the best buys are authentic, made using old hand- and woodblock-printing techniques.

Stores selling a host of fine silks, damasks, and other fabrics (➤ 80–81) reflect the city's trading days. And as you'd expect in a city with such an illustrious artistic past, antiques shops are filled with beautiful paintings, prints, and objets d'art (➤ 82).

MURANO GLASS

Made around Venice since Roman times, glassmaking took off in the 13th century, when foundries were moved to Murano (➤ 82) to eliminate the risk of fire. Today, the island is a key production center; though stores sell Murano glass everywhere in Venice, the best choice, and keenest prices, are on the island. With its ornate forms and many colors Murano glass is an acquired taste but the huge variety of styles include both contemporary and traditional designs. At its best, glass is one of the city's most distinctive buys.

Out and About

Above left to right: *a visit to Venice would not be complete without a trip aboard a gondola;*
the island of Murano, famous for its glass and its elegant clocktower;
no, it's not art—it's a house in Burano;
the peaceful canalside on the island of Torcello

INFORMATION

Murano

✚ H4–N7

🚤 42 (frequent) or 12 (every 60–90 mins) from Fondamente Nuove; journey takes about 8 mins

Museo Vetrario

☎ 041 739586

🕐 Thu–Tue 10–4:30 (winter 10–3:30)

💶 Moderate

Santa Maria e Donato

☎ 041 739056

🕐 Daily 9–noon, 4–6

💶 Free

ORGANIZED SIGHTSEEING

Although several firms offer sightseeing tours, the best trips are arranged by American Express (✉ Salizzada San Moisè, San Marco ☎ 041 520 0844). They offer two city tours daily, one in the morning and the other in the afternoon. The tours last two hours and cost around 22 euros; L42,000 for morning tours (year-round Mon–Sat) and 26 euros; L50,000 for afternoon tours (Mar–Oct only), with a reduction if you book both. The morning tour visits, among other sights, the Basilica di San Marco, the Campanile, and the Palazzo Ducale. The afternoon tour takes you to several palaces and churches, including the Frari, and ends at the Rialto bridge after a gondola ride to the Ca' d'Oro. Trips start from outside the American Express office; call ahead to confirm current prices and timings. American Express can organize multilingual guides for hire by the day, as well as gondoliers, or you can choose one yourself by contacting the Guides' Association (✉ Calle Morosini della Regina, 750 San Marco ☎ 041 520 9038).

ISLAND EXCURSIONS
Murano

Murano, a glass-making center since 1291, has three major sights over and above its ubiquitous glass workshops and showrooms. The first is the church of San Pietro Martire noted for Giovanni Bellini's altarpiece. Also well worth seeing is the Museo Vetrario, Italy's only glass museum, with displays of objects dating from Roman times. Just beyond lies the church of Santa Maria

e Donato, distinguished by a striking arched and colonnaded apse. Inside, the 12th-century apse mosaic of the Madonna is outstanding, as are the swirling colored patterns of the lovely mosaic floor (1141).

BURANO

In the Scuola (or Museo) dei Merletti you can see breathtaking intricate examples of traditional lace and watch local women working according to age-old methods. The island's fame in part rests on its many brightly painted houses, whose wonderful primary colors make its streets and canals as picturesque as Venice itself. Fishing boats moor at the island's fringes and nets are laid out to dry on the sidewalks, and despite the faint air of commercialism and the many visitors, the island feels like a genuine fishing community.

TORCELLO

One of the most magical places in Venice, Torcello was probably the city's birthplace and the first area of the lagoon settled in the 5th century. Malaria and the silting up of its canals snuffed out its prosperity in the 12th century, and today it is home to little more than a single hamlet and a beautiful patchwork of green fields and leafy canals dominated by the cathedral of Santa Maria Assunta, Venice's oldest building (founded 639) and one of its loveliest sights as well as the finest Veneto-Byzantine church in Italy. Climb the bell-tower for wonderful lagoon views. Also worth seeing close by are the Byzantine church of Santa Fosca and the small Museo di Torcello.

INFORMATION

BURANO
✚ H1–N2
🚤 12 from Fondamente Nuove, every 60–90 mins; journey takes 40–50 mins
Scuola dei Merletti
☎ 041 730034
🕐 Wed–Mon 10–5 (Nov–Mar 10–4)
♿ Moderate

TORCELLO
✚ Off map
🚤 12 from Fondamente Nuove, every 60–90 mins; journey takes 45 mins. Catch the first boat of the day to avoid the crowds
Santa Maria Assunta/Santa Fosca
☎ 041 730084
🕐 Daily 10–12:30, 2–5
♿ Inexpensive; Santa Fosca free
Museo di Torcello
☎ 041 730761
🕐 Winter: Tue–Sun 10–5. Summer Tue–Sun 10:30–6
♿ Inexpensive

21

Walks

INFORMATION

Distance 1.8 miles (0.9 miles to San Nicolò, 0.9 miles to the Salute)
Time 2–5 hours
Start point ★ Ponte di Rialto
➕ G11
🚤 Rialto 1, 3, 82
End point Piazza San Marco
➕ G12
🚤 Vallaresso 1, 3, 4, 82
🍴 Campo Santa Margherita, Campo San Polo, and Campo Santo Stefano (Campo Francesco Morosini)
(► 56–57)

0   600 m
0   600 yards

FROM THE RIALTO TO PIAZZA SAN MARCO

Walk north from the Rialto bridge up Ruga degli Orefici. Turn left on Ruga Vecchia San Giovanni and follow it west to Campo San Polo. From the square's southwestern corner follow the alleys to Campo San Tomà. From here, head to Campo dei Frari and follow Calle Scaleter and Calle San Pantalon to Campo San Pantalon and Campo Santa Margherita. From the latter, either walk to Campo San Barnaba along Rio Terrà Canal, or loop west from Campo dei Carmini to take in San Sebastiano and perhaps San Nicolò dei Mendicoli. Return to Campo San Barnaba on Calle d'Avogaria and Calle Lunga San Barnaba, then follow Calle dei Casini and Calle della Toletta to the Accademia. Here you might divert south to the Zattere ai Gesuati and then east to Punta della Dogana, returning to the Accademia via Santa Maria della Salute. Otherwise, if you cross the Ponte dell'Accademia you will reach Campo Santo Stefano (Campo Francesco Morosini).

Walk east on Calle Spezier into Campo San Maurizio. Continue east to Campo San Moisè via Campo Santa Maria Zobenigo and Calle Larga (Viale) XXII Marzo. Beyond San Moisè, turn right down Calle Vallaresso and follow the waterfront east to Piazza San Marco.

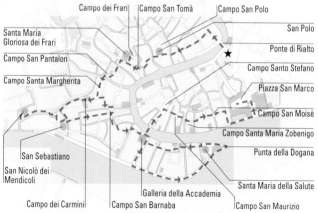

Campo dei Frari | Campo San Tomà | Campo San Polo

Santa Maria Gloriosa dei Frari

San Polo

Campo San Pantalon

Ponte di Rialto ★

Campo Santa Margherita

Campo Santo Stefano

Piazza San Marco

Campo San Moisè

Campo Santa Maria Zobenigo

Punta della Dogana

San Sebastiano

San Nicolò dei Mendicoli

Santa Maria della Salute

Galleria della Accademia | Campo San Barnaba | Campo San Maurizio

Campo dei Carmini

FROM PIAZZA SAN MARCO THROUGH THE CITY'S NORTHERN DISTRICTS TO THE JEWISH QUARTER

Walk east from Piazza San Marco to Campo di San Zaccaria. From the northwest corner of Campo di San Zaccaria, take Calle San Provolo north and then turn left on to Corte Rotta to reach Campo Santa Maria Formosa. Take Calle Lunga Santa Maria Formosa to the east and follow it to Calle Ospedale and Salizzada Santi Giovanni e Paolo. Turn left to reach Campo di Santi Giovanni e Paolo. Proceed west on Calle Larga G Gallina to Campo Santa Maria Nova, detouring south to Santa Maria dei Miracoli.

Continue northwest through Campo San Canciano. Shortly before reaching Campo Santi Apostoli, turn right on Calle Muazzo and Rio Terrà dei Santi Apostoli toward Campo dei Gesuiti. Turn left to follow Fondamenta Zen west along the canal. Turn left at the end (Calle della Racchetta) and then take the third right (Sottopasseggio dei Preti). Turn right on Fondamenta di San Felice, then left onto Fondamenta della Misericordia. At Calle Larga turn right to Campo dei Mori and Madonna dell'Orto. Return south to Fondamenta degli Ormesini and cross the Rio della Misericordia canal to reach Campo di Ghetto Nuovo, the heart of Venice's fascinating old Jewish ghetto.

INFORMATION

Distance 2 miles
Time 2–4 hours
Start point ★ Piazza San Marco
➕ G12
🚤 Vallaresso 1, 3, 4, 82
End point Campo di Ghetto Nuovo
➕ E9
🚤 Ponte Guglie 52
🍴 Campo Santa Maria Formosa (➤ 57)

0	600 m
0	600 yards

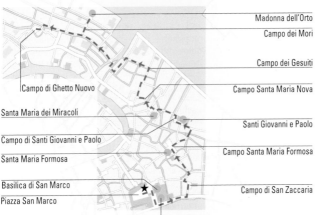

Madonna dell'Orto

Campo dei Mori

Campo dei Gesuiti

Campo di Ghetto Nuovo

Campo Santa Maria Nova

Santa Maria dei Miracoli

Santi Giovanni e Paolo

Campo di Santi Giovanni e Paolo

Campo Santa Maria Formosa

Santa Maria Formosa

Basilica di San Marco

Campo di San Zaccaria

Piazza San Marco

Palazzo Ducale

Venice by Night

Above: *darkness falls over the Grand Canal—an unforgettable sight*
Above right: *the Rialto bridge, spanning the Grand Canal, epitomizes the timeless elegance of Venice*

DARK WATERS

Few things are more enchanting than a trip down the Grand Canal under a starlit sky. Indeed, it is almost worth organizing your arrival in the city for nightfall, so that you can approach your hotel by *vaporetto* or water taxi under the cover of darkness: it may be the most memorable part of your trip. And if you are going to lavish a small fortune on a gondola ride, make sure it is at night. Better still, make sure it is also in the silent, dark-dappled canals away from the main waterways.

If Venice is beautiful beyond words by day, then it is still more sublime by night. With the day-trippers gone, the students, shoppers, and other day-time stragglers mysteriously vanished, most streets and alleys are eerily quiet. The gentle lap of the water is often the only sound, occasionally broken by a distant footfall, the splash of a gondolier's oar, or the call of cats on their nocturnal prowl. This is the time for assignations, strolls, and nightcaps in fusty, wooden-beamed bars. Wherever you walk you are rewarded by a fairy-tale world of medieval corners and views all the more magical for the cover of night. Much the same goes for Venice's watery domain, which is doubly enchanting on sultry summer evenings.

You need not fear for your personal security—Venice is very safe. You won't find clubs, pubs, and thumping music: the city goes to bed remarkably early—one reason for the magical quiet of the streets. If you want some life, however, and the promise of an aperitif at the end of your stroll, you will find the odd late-night bar or evening recital, particularly around Campo Santa Margherita—and the city's opera and Casino are both night-time favorites—but such diversions are the exception rather than the rule. Venice is a city where the received wisdom is that it's impossible to escape the crowds but Venice by night is when the city is returned to itself, and when you can pretend, should you wish, that you are all but alone in the most beautiful place on earth. (For further after-dark entertainment ➤ 84–85.)

VENICE's
top 25 sights

The sights are shown on the maps on the inside front cover and inside back cover, numbered **1**–**25** across the city

Canal Grande

HIGHLIGHTS

- Palazzo Vendramin-Calergi (➤ 59)
- San Stae
- Ca' Pesaro (➤ 59)
- Ca' d'Oro (➤ 37)
- Ponte di Rialto (➤ 58)

INFORMATION

Regata Storica

There's no better introduction to the magic of Venice than a boat trip down the Grand Canal. The world's most beautiful "street" offers an endlessly unfolding pageant with superb views of the city's finest palaces and a fascinating insight into Venetian life.

A riot of color and noise Snaking 2.5 miles through the heart of Venice, it divides the city: three of the city's six districts, or *sestieri*, lie to one side and three to the other. At most hours of the day and night it is alive with boats and bustle, providing an almost hypnotic spectacle when admired from one of its three bridges (the Scalzi, Rialto, and Accademia) or from the heavily laden *vaporetti* that ply up and down its length. In addition to the life of the canal is the attraction of the palaces that line its banks, an historical digest of the city's most appealing architecture dating back over 500 years.

Jump on board A trip along this intriguing canal is a pleasure in itself, and one that you can never tire of. Board either *vaporetto* No. 1 or No. 82 at Piazzale Roma or the Ferrovia (railway station), making sure the boat is heading in the right direction. For the best views, try to secure one of the few outside seats at the front or rear of the boat: Venetians prefer to stand in the middle. The Rialto and Accademia bridges make convenient breaks in the ride, but for your first trip stay aboard all the way to San Marco (and then do the return trip to take in the splendor of the palaces on the opposite bank). It is also well worth making the trip at night, when the experience, if anything, is even more magical.

San Sebastiano

While paintings by some of Venice's artists—notably Titian and Tintoretto—are often showcased in grandiose settings, the city's finest collection of works by Veronese is gathered in the humble little church of San Sebastiano.

Veronese Born in Verona, Paolo Caliari Veronese (1528–88) moved to Venice while he was in his twenties, settling close to San Sebastiano, which became his parish church. In 1555 he was commissioned to decorate the sacristy, where he left paintings of the *Evangelists* and the *Coronation of the Virgin*. Impressed by his work, the church authorities gave him free rein to decorate the ceiling, and he produced a sumptuous collection of paintings, gilt, and elaborate stucco (much of the decoration was by Veronese's brother, Benedetto). The three main panels depict episodes from the story of Esther, chosen for its symbolic parallels with the stories of Eve and the Virgin Mary.

Monopoly The hand of Veronese can also be seen in the choir, where he painted the high altarpiece—the *Madonna and Child with Sts. Sebastian, Peter, Francis, and Catherine* (1570)—and the two vast paintings on the north and south walls. The latter portray *Sts. Mark and Marcellinus Led to Martyrdom and Comforted by St. Sebastian* and *The Second Martyrdom of St. Sebastian* (Sebastian survived his first assault by arrows and was martyred by being pummeled to death). Veronese also painted *The Trial and Martyrdom of St. Sebastian* in the nuns' choir, an unusual gallery above the church's west end. He even designed the organ and painted its door panels, his decorative monopoly of San Sebastiano making it only fitting that he was buried here: his tomb, and that of his brother, lie in front of the chapel.

HIGHLIGHTS

- Sacristy
- Ceiling
- Nuns' choir
- Choir
- Organ
- *St. Nicholas* (1563), Titian (first chapel on right)
- *Madonna and Child* (16th century), Tommaso Lombardo (second chapel on right)
- *Tomb of Archbishop Podocattaro of Cyprus* (d1555), Sansovino (fourth chapel on right)

INFORMATION

- C13; Locator map A4
- Campo San Sebastiano
- 041 282487 or 041 275 0462
- Mon–Sat 10–5
- Campo Santa Margherita and Campo San Barnaba
- San Basilio 82
- Good
- Inexpensive
- Scuola Grande dei Carmini (➤ 28), Scuola Grande di San Rocco (➤ 29), Santa Maria Gloriosa dei Frari (➤ 30), Ca' Rezzonico (➤ 31), Gallerie dell'Accademia (➤ 33)

Scuola Grande dei Carmini

Giovanni Battista Tiepolo's paintings are not to all tastes, but those in the intimate Scuola Grande dei Carmini— all pastel shades and fleshy figures— are a pleasant change from the more obvious drama of Titian or Tintoretto.

Carmelites The Carmelite Order's Venetian chapter was originally installed in Santa Maria del Carmelo (or Carmini), the Carmelite church just to the left of the *scuola* (see below). In 1667 the order commissioned Baldassare Longhena, one of the era's leading architects, to design a new home in the present building (Longhena also designed Santa Maria della Salute and a number of palaces on the Grand Canal). The facade, though hampered by its cramped site, is known for its rigorous symmetry and many masks and projections, all favored by architects of the period.

Exuberant ceilings The highlights are Giovanni Battista Tiepolo's nine ceiling paintings (1739–44) in the Salone, a large room on the second floor reached via an extravagantly stuccoed staircase. The paintings' central panel depicts the vision of St. Simon Stock elected the Carmelites' prior-general in 1247, in which the Virgin appears to the saint with a "scapular." This garment of two linked pieces of cloth became central to Carmelite belief as wearers were promised relief from the pains of purgatory on the "first Sunday after death." Two adjacent rooms, the Albergo and Archivio, have heavy wooden ceilings and several paintings, the best of which is Piazzetta's *Judith and Holofernes* (1743). Be sure to visit the adjacent Chiesa dei Carmini to see Lorenzo Lotto's *St. Nicholas of Bari* (1529), located by the side door (second chapel), and Cima da Conegliano's fine *Nativity* (1509) above the second altar on the opposite (south) wall.

Scuola Grande di San Rocco

In a city of superlative and often striking works of art, there can be few that make such a marked and powerful first impression than the colossal cycle of 54 paintings by Tintoretto that line the walls here.

From rags to riches This *scuola*, formerly a charitable institution for the sick, was founded in 1478 in honor of St. Roch, a saint whose efficacy against disease made him popular in pestilence-ridden Venice. In 1564, having become one of the city's wealthiest fraternities, the *scuola* instigated a competition to decorate the walls of its meeting place. It was won by Tintoretto, who then spent some 23 years creating one of Europe's greatest painting cycles.

The wonders inside To see Tintoretto's 54 paintings in the order they were painted, ignore the canvases on the first floor and in the main hall (Sala Grande) up the stairs. Instead, go to the Sala dell'Albergo (off the main hall), dominated by a huge *Crucifixion* (1565), often described as one of Italy's greatest paintings. The room's central ceiling panel is *St. Roch in Glory*, the painting that won Tintoretto his commission. In the main hall are ceiling paintings (1575–81) describing episodes from the Old Testament, all carefully chosen to draw parallels with the *scuola*'s charitable or curative aims. The ten wall paintings show scenes from the New Testament. Note the superb 17th-century wooden carvings around the walls, by the little-known sculptor Francesco Pianta. Of the eight paintings downstairs, the artist's last in the *scuola* (1583–88), the best are the idiosyncratic *Annunciation* and *The Flight into Egypt*.

HIGHLIGHTS

- *Crucifixion*
- *Moses Strikes Water from the Rock*
- *The Fall of Manna*
- *The Temptation of Christ*
- *The Adoration of the Shepherds*
- *Wooden sculptures*
- *The Flight into Egypt*
- *Annunciation*

Tintoretto's Crucifixion

INFORMATION

- ⊞ E11; Locator map B3
- ✉ Campo San Rocco
- ☎ 041 523 4864; www.sanrocco.it
- ⊙ May–Oct: daily 9–5:30. Nov–Apr: daily 10–4
- ∥ Campo dei Frari
- ⊟ San Tomà 1, 82
- ♿ Poor
- 💷 Moderate
- ↔ San Sebastiano (► 27), Scuola Grande dei Carmini (► 28), Santa Maria Gloriosa dei Frari (► 30)
- ❓ A leaflet about the *scuola*'s paintings is usually available with your ticket

29

Santa Maria Gloriosa dei Frari

HIGHLIGHTS

- *Madonna and Child*, Giovanni Bellini
- *Assumption*, Titian
- *Madonna di Ca' Pesaro*, Titian
- *Madonna and Child* (1339), Paolo Veneziano (sacristy)
- *St. John the Baptist*, Donatello
- *Mausoleo Tiziano* (Tomb of Titian)
- *Monumento a Iacopo Marcello* (d1484)
- Wooden choir (124 stalls)
- *Monumento al Doge Giovanni Pesaro*
- *Monumento al Canova*

INFORMATION

- ✚ E11; Locator map B3
- ✉ Campo dei Frari
- ☎ 041 522 2637
- 🕐 Mon–Sat 9–6; Sun 1–6
- 🍴 Campo dei Frari
- 🚤 San Tomà 1, 82
- ♿ Good: one or two steps
- 💷 Inexpensive; free on Sun
- ↔ San Sebastiano (➤ 27), Scuola Grande dei Carmini (➤ 28), Scuola Grande di San Rocco (➤ 29), Ca' Rezzonico (➤ 31), Gallerie dell'Accademia (➤ 33)

If you were allowed to walk away with just one work of art from Venice it could well be Bellini's sublime altarpiece in this church—although two other paintings in this magnificent Gothic church are contenders.

Magnificent edifice The Frari narrowly outranks Santi Giovanni e Paolo as Venice's largest and most important church. Founded around 1250, it became the mother church of the city's Franciscans, after whom it is named—*frari* is a Venetian corruption of *frati*, meaning "friars."

The greats interred Many of the city's great and good are buried in the church, among them the painter Titian (d1576), whose 19th-century tomb occupies the second altar on the right (south) wall. Opposite, on the left wall, stands the *Monumento al Canova* (1827), an unmistakable marble pyramid that contains the sculptor's heart. To its right lies the wonderfully gaudy tomb of Doge Giovanni Pesaro (d1659). The composer Claudio Monteverdi (d1643) is buried in the third chapel to the left of the high altar.

Art The Frari's most striking painting is Titian's *Assumption* (1516–18), its position above the high altar designed to attract your attention from most of the church. The same painter's influential *Madonna di Ca' Pesaro* (1526), on the last altar of the left aisle, is almost equally captivating. The most beautiful work of art in the church, however, is Giovanni Bellini's sublime triptych of the *Madonna and Child between Sts. Nicholas, Peter, Mark and Benedict* (1488), located in the sacristy off the right transept. In the first chapel on the right of the high altar is Donatello's statue of *St. John the Baptist* (1438), the only work in Venice by the famous Florentine sculptor.

Ca' Rezzonico

Gazing at the Grand Canal's palaces from a boat you can't help but wish to see inside some of them, which is the attraction of Ca' Rezzonico, a museum that recreates a Venetian palace as it might have been in the 18th century.

How it began The Ca' Rezzonico was begun in 1667 by Baldassare Longhena, one of the leading architects of his day, but remained half-finished following the ruin of its owner, Filippo Bon. In 1751 the shell was bought by the Rezzonico family, a *nouveau riche* clan, and then passed through several hands, including the son of poet Robert Browning, before opening as a museum in 1936. It begins in fine style with a sumptuous ballroom done with *trompe-l'œil* and enormous chandeliers. Highlights of subsequent rooms include ceiling frescoes by G.B. Tiepolo, some fine lacquerwork, Flemish tapestries, and pastel portraits by Rosalba Carriera.

The collection Much of the palace's third floor is devoted to a picture gallery, whose highlight is a pair of paintings by Canaletto, two of only a handful that remain on public display in Venice. Also of interest are Francesco Guardi's views of the city's convents and gambling rooms, together with 34 amateurish but fascinating portraits of Venetian life by Pietro Longhi, among them his well-known *Rhinoceros*, painted during the animal's stay in Venice in 1779. Rooms off to the right include a splendid bed-chamber, complete with 18th-century closet and sponge-bag. The final rooms contain the museum's pictorial high point, a series of satirical frescoes (1793–97) by G.D. Tiepolo. The fourth floor offers puppets, a reconstructed 18th-century pharmacy, and fine views.

HIGHLIGHTS

- Ballroom
- G.B. Tiepolo ceiling frescoes
- Carriera portraits
- Lacquerwork
- Gondola cabin, or *felze* (first floor)
- Canaletto paintings
- Francesco Guardi paintings
- Pietro Longhi paintings
- G.D. Tiepolo satirical frescoes

INFORMATION

- E12; Locator map B3
- Fondamenta Rezzonico
- 041 241 0100
- Wed–Mon 10–6
- Campo San Barnaba
- Ca' Rezzonico 1
- Good
- Expensive
- San Sebastiano (➤ 27), Scuola Grande dei Carmini (➤ 28), Scuola Grande di San Rocco (➤ 29), Santa Maria Gloriosa dei Frari (➤ 30), Gallerie dell'Accademia (➤ 33), Collezione Peggy Guggenheim (➤ 34)

A gondola cabin, or felze

Santo Stefano

Savor the sensation of walking from the heat and bustle of a city into a building that induces immediate calm, an effect that is soon gained by the soothing Gothic interior of this, one of Venice's loveliest churches.

Ideally placed Santo Stefano sits on the edge of Campo Santo Stefano (also known as Campo Francesco Morosini), one of Venice's most charming squares; the nearby Paolin is an ideal place to sit with a drink or ice-cream (▶ 77). The church has not always been so peaceful, having been reconsecrated six times to wash away the stain of blood spilled by murders within its walls. Today, its interior is overarched by an exquisite "ship's keel" ceiling and framed by tie beams and pillars of Greek and red Veronese marble.

Final resting place At the center of the nave lies Doge Francesco Morosini (*d*1612, and buried under Venice's largest tomb slab), famous for recapturing the Peloponnese and blowing up the Parthenon with a single shot. Other tombs command attention, notably Pietro Lombardo's *Monument to Giacomo Surian* (*d*1493) on the wall to the right of the main door, but the church's chief artistic interest lies in the gloomy sacristy at the end of the right nave. The altar wall displays two narrow-framed *Saints* by Bartolomeo Vivarini, as well as a recessed 13th-century Byzantine icon. On the walls to either side are four paintings by Tintoretto and four portraits of Augustinian cardinals (Santo Stefano is an Augustinian church).

The leaning bell tower of Santo Stefano

Gallerie dell'Accademia

An art gallery is almost superfluous in a city where art awaits you at every turn, but you would miss a key experience without a visit to the Accademia, home to the world's greatest collection of Venetian paintings.

History The Accademia began life as Venice's art school in 1750, moving to its present site in 1807 when it garnered much of its permanent collection from churches and religious houses suppressed by Napoleonic decree. Its paintings, arranged chronologically, spread across 24 rooms.

Masterpieces Some of the gallery's best-known paintings are found in the first five rooms, Room 1 opening with Byzantine works, a style that influenced the city's earliest painters. Rooms 2 to 5 contain canvases by Carpaccio, Mantegna, Bellini, and others, reflecting Venice's Renaissance heyday, as well as the Accademia's most famous painting, Giorgione's mysterious *Tempest* (*c*1500). Rooms 10 and 11 have High Renaissance masterpieces, such as Veronese's luxuriant *Supper in the House of Levi* (1573) and Tintoretto's iconoclastic *Miracle of the Slave* and *The Translation of the Body of St. Mark* (*c*1560).

Cycles Leave plenty of time for the Accademia's highlights, two *storie*, or fresco cycles (Rooms 20 and 21). The first, "The Miracles of the True Cross" (1494–1510), was painted by a variety of artists for the Scuola di San Giovanni Evangelista. Each describes a miracle worked by a relic of the "True Cross" owned by the *scuola*, though often the miracle itself takes second place to the fascinating anecdotal detail. The same is true for the second cycle, painted by Carpaccio for the Scuola di Sant'Orsola, with episodes from the "Life of St. Ursula."

HIGHLIGHTS

- *Coronation of the Virgin* (*c*1345), Paolo Veneziano (Room 1)
- *Presentation of Jesus in the Temple*, Carpaccio (Room 2)
- *Madonna and Saints* (*c*1485), Giovanni Bellini (Room 2)
- *Tempest*, Giorgione (Room 5)
- *Supper in the House of Levi*, Veronese (Room 10)
- *The Translation of the Body of St. Mark*, Tintoretto (Room 10)
- *Pietà* (*c*1576), Titian (Room 10)
- Pietro Longhi paintings (Room 17)
- "The Miracles of the True Cross" (Room 20)
- "Life of St. Ursula" (*c*1490– 96), Carpaccio (Room 21)

INFORMATION

- ⊞ E13; Locator map B4
- ✉ Campo della Carità
- ☎ 041 522 2247
- ◷ Tue–Sun 8:15–7:15, Mon 8:15–2
- ▮▮ Campo Santo Stefano
- ⊟ Accademia 1, 3, 4, 82
- ⎣ Poor: some steps
- 🎟 Expensive
- ↔ Santo Stefano (▶ 32), Collezione Peggy Guggenheim (▶ 34)
- ❓ Arrive early to avoid lines

33

Collezione Peggy Guggenheim

HIGHLIGHTS

- Garden
- The New Wing
- Henry Moore sculptures
- *Bird in Space*, Constantin Brancusi
- *Red Tower*, De Chirico
- *Robing of the Bride*, Max Ernst
- Silver bedhead, Alexander Calder
- Jackson Pollock paintings
- *The Poet*, Pablo Picasso
- *Angel of the Citadel*, Marino Marini

INFORMATION

- ✚ F13; Locator map C4
- ✉ Palazzo Venier dei Leoni, Calle San Cristoforo
- ☎ 041 520 6288
- ◷ Apr–Oct: Wed–Mon 10–6 (Sat until 10). Nov–Mar: Wed–Mon 10–6
- 🛥 Salute 1
- ♿ Good
- 💷 Expensive
- ↔ Ca' Rezzonico (➤ 31), Santo Stefano (➤ 32), Gallerie dell'Accademia (➤ 33), Santa Maria della Salute (➤ 36)

It's rather apt that the Accademia and Guggenheim, Venice's two most visited galleries, are so close together, juxtaposing two matchless collections of paintings and sculptures—one traditional and one modern.

Perfect setting The Guggenheim's small but polished collection was accumulated by Peggy Guggenheim (1898–1979), daughter of an American copper magnate, and installed by her in the 18th-century Palazzo Venier dei Leoni. The collection's appeal owes much to its immaculate presentation as well as to the beauty of its setting, many of the sculptures being arranged in a lovely garden. This has works by Henry Moore, Paolozzi, Giacometti, and others, and houses the New Wing and appealing "Museum Store."

Modern art Guggenheim's taste and money allowed her to select high-quality works from virtually every modern-art movement of the 20th century. At the same time she had a penchant for the surreal and avant-garde, having enjoyed a brief relationship with the Surrealist painter Max Ernst. The collection features Cubist works by Picasso and Braque, and the Surrealism of Dalí, Magritte, and Miró. American modernists include Jackson Pollock and Rothko, while the English are represented by Francis Bacon. There are also sculptures by Calder and Brancusi, as well as works by Italian Futurists Balla and Boccioni. The most memorable work is Marino Marini's provocative *Angel of the Citadel*, on the terrace overlooking the Grand Canal.

Angel of the Citadel

Madonna dell'Orto

Madonna dell'Orto ranks high among the many superb Venetian churches; its lovely setting well off the tourist trail and graceful red-brick facade are complemented by an airy interior filled with appealing works of art.

Exterior The first church on the present site was founded in 1350 and dedicated to St. Christopher, a statue of whom still dominates the lovely brick and marble facade. The sculpture was commissioned by the Merchants' Guild, whose altar to the saint (their patron) lay within the church. The building was rededicated to the Virgin in 1377, an act that was inspired by a miracle-working statue of the Madonna found in a nearby vegetable garden (*orto*). The elegant doorway, by Bartolomeo Bon, is a Renaissance-tinged work that departs from the facade's predominantly Gothic inspiration. Note the onion dome of the campanile, clear witness to the Byzantine influence on Venetian architecture.

Interior splendor The artistic highlights begin above the first altar on the right, which has Cima da Conegliano's *St. John the Baptist* (1493). At the end of the right nave, above the door, stands Tintoretto's dramatic *Presentation of the Virgin* (1551). In the chapel to the right of the choir lies Tintoretto's tomb, together with those of his children, Domenico and Marietta, both painters themselves (Madonna dell'Orto was the family's parish church). A wall separates the artist from two of his finest paintings, the choir's grand *Last Judgment* and *The Making of the Golden Calf*. Of the three paintings in the apse to the rear, those on the right and left—the *Beheading of St. Paul* and *St. Peter's Vision of the Cross*—are by Tintoretto; the central *Annunciation* is by Palma il Giovane. Four of the five *Virtues* above are also by Tintoretto.

HIGHLIGHTS

- Facade
- Doorway
- *St. Christopher*, Nicolò di Giovanni
- Campanile
- *St. John the Baptist*, Cima da Conegliano
- *Presentation of the Virgin*, Tintoretto
- *The Making of the Golden Calf*, Tintoretto
- *Last Judgement*, Tintoretto
- *St. Agnes Raising Licinius*, Tintoretto (Cappella Contarini)

INFORMATION

- F8–9; Locator map C1
- Campo Madonna dell'Orto
- 041 719933 or 041 275 0462
- Mon–Sat 10–5
- Madonna dell'Orto 41, 42, 51, 52
- Good
- Inexpensive
- Ca' d'Oro (➤ 37)

Red-brick facade of the Madonna dell'Orto

35

Santa Maria della Salute

HIGHLIGHTS

INFORMATION

The Salute's interior

In a city where almost every street and canal offers a memorable vista, this church, proudly situated at the entrance to the Grand Canal, forms part of the panorama most people readily associate with Venice.

Plague In 1630 Venice found itself ravaged by a plague so severe that the Senate promised to build a church in honor of the Virgin if she could save the city. Within weeks the pestilence had abated, and on April 1 the following year the first stone of the Salute, meaning "health" and "salvation" in Italian, was laid. Its architect, chosen after a competition, was Baldassare Longhena, responsible for a host of outstanding Venetian buildings. His design proved to be a baroque model for years to come, combining the Palladian influence of his master, Scamozzi (Palladio's closest follower), with a range of personal innovations.

Baroque interior The Salute's main impact is as a distant prospect, its dazzling exterior detail and great dome (modeled on that of St. Peter's in Rome) forming irreplaceable elements of the Venetian skyline. The church's interior is more restrained, and its fine marble floor is the first thing that catches your eye. Moving left from the side entrance, the third of the three altars boasts an early painting by Titian, the *Descent of the Holy Spirit* (1550). The high altar supports *The Virgin Casting out the Plague* (1670), a magnificent sculpture designed by Longhena and carved by Juste le Court. The supplicant figure on the left represents Venice, while the elderly harridan moving off to the right symbolizes the plague. It is well worth paying the entrance fee for the sacristy, which contains paintings by Titian and Tintoretto.

Ca' d'Oro

The smaller and less famous galleries of a city are often more rewarding than some of the bigger attractions. The Ca' d'Oro's collection of paintings, sculptures, and objets d'art is one of the most absorbing in Venice.

Palace The Ca' d'Oro, or "House of Gold," takes its name from the gilding that once covered its facade, a decorative veneer now worn away by wind and rain. The facade remains one of the most accomplished pieces of Venetian-Byzantine architecture in the city. The same, sadly, cannot be said of the interior, which has been ravaged by a succession of hapless owners. The palace was handed over to the state in 1916.

Exhibits The gallery divides into two floors, each of these arranged around a central *portego* On the second floor a captivating polyptych of the *Crucifixion* by Antonio Vivarini greets you, along with sculptural fragments belonging to the *Massacre of the Innocents* (14th century). Moving right you come to the gallery's pictorial masterpiece, Mantegna's somber *St. Sebastian* (1506). To its left, in the *portego*, is a pair of busts by Tullio Lombardo (15th century), followed by six bronze reliefs by Andrea Briscio (1470–1532). Rooms off the *portego* contain medallions, a *Madonna* by Giovanni Bellini, and Florentine and Sienese paintings. Upstairs are tapestries, paintings by Titian, Van Dyck, and Tintoretto, and damaged frescoes by Pordenone, Titian, and Giorgione.

HIGHLIGHTS

- Grand Canal facade
- *Massacre of the Innocents*, artist unknown
- *Crucifixion*, Antonio Vivarini
- Three-dimensional *paliotto* with *Scenes from the Life of St. Catherine* (16th century), artist unknown
- *St. Sebastian*, Andrea Mantegna
- *Man* and *Woman*, busts by Tullio Lombardo
- *The Story of the True Cross*, bronze reliefs by Andrea Briscio
- *Madonna of the Beautiful Eyes*, Giovanni Bellini
- *Flagellation*, Luca Signorelli
- *Scenes from the Life of Lucrezia*, Biagio d'Antonio

The Ca' d'Oro's ornate facade

INFORMATION

- F10; Locator map C2
- Calle di Ca' d'Oro, off Strada Nova
- 041 523 8790
- Mon 8:15–2; Tue–Sun 8:15–7:15
- Strada Nova
- Ca' d'Oro 1
- Poor: stairs to upper floors
- Moderate
- Madonna dell'Orto (► 35), Santa Maria dei Miracoli (► 43), Santi Giovanni e Paolo (► 45)

37

Piazza San Marco

INFORMATION

Avoid visiting Piazza San Marco on your first morning as the crowds might turn you against Venice. Once you've acquired a taste for the city you'll be ready to venture into one of the world's most famous squares.

Hordes Europe's "drawing-room" was how Napoleon described Venice's main square, though glancing at its present-day summer crowds he would probably be less complimentary. The piazza is too crowded, but early in the morning or off-season its considerable charms can still work their spell. The area was initially planted with an orchard belonging to the nuns of nearby San Zaccaria. Before the building of the Basilica, Campanile, and Palazzo Ducale—the square's most famous sights—it was home to a lighthouse and a pair of churches. Its 1,000-year transformation began in the 9th century, when the nuns sacrificed their trees to make way for the Basilica and Palazzo Ducale. The 12th century saw the arrival of the Procuratie, built to house Venice's civil servants, followed in the 16th century by the Zecca (Mint) and Libreria Sansoviniana.

Sights Over and above the obvious sights and cafés, make a point of seeing the archaeological museum, the Torre dell'Orologio (1496–99), complete with zodiac and 24-hour clock-face, and the two granite columns that stand on the waterfront area in front of the Palazzo Ducale. One is topped with the lion of St. Mark, the other with St. Theodore and a beast of mysterious origin. The area was once a place of execution, hence it is considered unlucky to walk between the pillars. The Libreria Sansoviniana, designed by Sansovino, was considered one of the greatest buildings of its day—despite the fact that its ceiling came crashing down shortly after completion.

Museo Civico Correr

Probably only a fraction of the visitors thronging Piazza San Marco venture into the Museo Civico Correr. Those who do not are missing Venice's finest museum and picture gallery with a remarkable collection of paintings.

Fascinating overview Much of the Correr's collection was accumulated by Abbot Teodoro Correr, a Venetian worthy, and bequeathed to the city in 1830. Today, it spreads over three floors, devoted respectively to historical displays, an art gallery, and the small Museo del Risorgimento (this details the 19th-century unification of Italy). The key rooms have lovely old prints and paintings of the city, followed by salons devoted to different episodes of Venetian history. Particularly outstanding are the rooms of costumes and hats, standards, armor, globes, old weapons, and ships' instruments. Perhaps the most memorable section, however, is the footwear display showing the famous "platform" shoes once worn by Venetian ladies of rank.

More art One of the main sections of the museum consists of a large hall devoted to several fine sculptures by Antonio Canova. Look out, in particular, for the touching study of Daedalus fixing a pair of flimsy wings to Icarus's arms. Occupying the third floor is the city's second-finest art gallery after the Accademia. Its most popular picture is Carpaccio's *Two Women* (1507), a masterful study of *ennui* that was for many years known as *The Courtesans* after its protagonists' plunging necklines. Other well-known paintings include *The Man in the Red Hat* (by either Carpaccio or Lorenzo Lotto) and a *Pietà* by Antonello da Messina, together with works by Cosmè Tura, Alvise Vivarini, and Jacopo, Giovanni and Gentile Bellini.

HIGHLIGHTS

- Aerial view of Venice (1500), Jacopo de' Barbari
- *Daedalus and Icarus*, Canova
- *Two Women*, Carpaccio
- *The Man in the Red Hat*, Lorenzo Lotto (attributed)
- *Pietà*, Antonello da Messina
- *Madonna and Child*, Giovanni Bellini

Gentile Bellini's Doge Giovanni Mocenigo

INFORMATION

- ✚ G12; Locator map D3
- ✉ Procuratie Nuove, Ala Napoleonica, Piazza San Marco
- ☎ 041 522 5625
- 🕐 Apr–Oct: daily 9–7. Nov–Mar: daily 9–5.
- 🍴 Piazza San Marco
- 🚏 Vallaresso 1, 3, 4, 82
- ♿ Poor
- 💰 Expensive
- ↔ Piazza San Marco (► 38), Campanile (► 40), Basilica di San Marco (► 41)

Campanile

One look at the lines might be enough to put you off taking the elevator up the Campanile, but grit your teeth and wait in line, for the views from the top—stretching to the Alps on a clear day—are absolutely unforgettable.

Purpose Venice's tallest building (323 feet) was reputedly founded in 912 on April 25, the feast day of St. Mark. In its earliest role it served as a bell tower for the Basilica and as a lighthouse for the harbor below. Its summit was sheathed in bronze, designed to catch the sun's rays and act as a beacon during the day. Venetians had long trusted the Campanile's supposedly massive foundations, believed to fan out in a star-shaped bulwark below the piazza. In fact, they were just 66 feet deep, a design fault exacerbated over the centuries by wind, rain, and saltwater erosion, not to mention countless lightning strikes.

Collapse Disaster struck on July 14, 1902, when, after a few warning cracks, the 990-year-old Campanile collapsed gently to the ground in front of a bewildered crowd. Remarkably no one was hurt—the only casualty being the custodian's cat, which had returned to the evacuated tower to finish its breakfast. More remarkable still, the Basilica and Palazzo Ducale escaped virtually unscathed. Plans were immediately made to rebuild the tower *dov' era e com' era*—"where it was and how it was." The new Campanile was inaugurated on April 25, 1912, exactly 1,000 years after its predecessor—though this time 650 tons lighter and with an extra 1,000 foundation piles.

Basilica di San Marco

Don't allow yourself to be discouraged by the teeming crowds that engulf the Basilica di San Marco, as ultimately no one can remain unimpressed by what is surely one of the world's greatest medieval buildings.

St. Mark's resting place The Basilica was begun in 832 to house the body of St. Mark, stolen from Alexandria by Venetian merchants four years earlier. For almost a thousand years it served as the doge's private "chapel" and the city's spiritual heart, accumulating the decorative fruits of a millennium to emerge as the most exotic hybrid of Western and Byzantine architecture in Europe. The original building (destroyed by rioting) was replaced in 978 and again in 1094, the church from the latter date making up most of the one you see today.

Time to explore Admiring the Basilica's treasures is exhausting, partly because there are so many, and partly because the almost constant crowds make exploring a dispiriting business. Still, the building remains overwhelmingly striking; spend a few minutes taking in some of the exterior details before plunging inside. These include the *Translation of the Body of St. Mark to the Basilica* (1260–70) above the leftmost door, the west facade's only original mosaic (the rest are later copies), and the superb Romanesque carvings (1240–65) above the central door. Inside, see the famous bronze horses (probably 3rd century AD) in the Museo Marciano, the view from the Loggia dei Cavalli, the treasury (full of antique silverware), and the magnificent Pala d'Oro, an altar screen encrusted with over 2,600 pearls, rubies, emeralds, and other precious stones.

HIGHLIGHTS

- Central door
- Facade mosaics
- Bronze horses
- View from Loggia dei Cavalli
- Rood screen
- Mosaic pavement
- Treasury
- Madonna de Nicopeia
- Pala d'Oro
- Interior mosaics

INFORMATION

- ✚ G12–H12; Locator map D3
- ✉ Piazza San Marco
- ☎ 041 522 5205/5697
- 🕐 Summer: Mon–Sat 9:45–5; Sun 2–5. Winter: Mon–Sat 9:45–4; Sun 2–4
- 🍴 Piazza San Marco
- 🚢 Vallaresso or San Zaccaria 1, 52, 82
- ♿ Some steps; uneven floors
- 🎫 Basilica free. Museo Marciano, Treasury, and Pala d'Oro inexpensive
- ↔ Piazza San Marco (➤ 38), Campanile (➤ 40), Palazzo Ducale (➤ 42)

St. Mark's richly designed facade

41

Palazzo Ducale

HIGHLIGHTS

- Bridge of Sighs
- Tetrarchs
- Porta della Carta
- Scala dei Giganti
- Arco Foscari
- Sala dell'Anticollegio
- Sala del Collegio
- Sala del Maggior Consiglio
- Armory
- Prisons

INFORMATION

- H12; Locator map D3
- Piazzetta San Marco
- Palace 041 522 4951. Guided tours 041 520 4287
- Palace Apr–Oct: 9–7 (last ticket sold 5:30). Nov–Mar: 9–5 (last ticket sold 3:30).
- Piazza San Marco
- Vallaresso or San Zaccaria 1, 3, 4, 52, 82
- Poor: steps to upper floors
- Very expensive

Bridge of Sighs

Italy has a host of beautiful Gothic buildings, but the Palazzo Ducale is by far the most captivating: the ornate and many-roomed seat of the doge and home to Venice's various offices of state for almost a thousand years.

Evalution The first ducal palace, completed in 814, was a severe fortress built on one of the few clay redoubts in the lagoon. This burned down in 976, as did its successor in 1106. By 1419 the palace was in its third—and final—incarnation. Three years later, the great hall, or Sala del Maggior Consiglio, was completed—one of many additions made to the interior as the machinery of the state expanded. By 1550 most work had been completed, only to be undone by fires in 1574 and 1577, conflagrations that not only destroyed masterpieces by some of Venice's greatest painters, but also threatened the entire building with collapse. Restoration work continued on and off until the 1880s.

Details Outside, note the famous Ponte dei Sospiri (Bridge of Sighs), tucked down a canal at the palace's eastern end, and the fine sculptures on each of the building's three corners. Also take in the excellent carving of the pillars and capitals, and the palace's superb main doorway, the Porta della Carta (1438–43), together with the famous little group of red porphyry knights, or tetrarchs, to its left. Beyond the courtyard and ticket office an ornate staircase leads up several flights to the beginning of the palace's set itinerary, a marked route leading from one lavishly designed room to the next. Look for works by Tintoretto, Veronese, and other Venetian masters, in particular Tintoretto's gargantuan *Paradiso* (1588–92), the world's largest oil painting, in the Sala del Maggior Consiglio.

Santa Maria dei Miracoli

You'll soon get used to being brought up short in Venice by surprises and views around almost every corner, but none quite compares with a first glimpse of the beautiful multicolored marbles of Santa Maria dei Miracoli.

Miracles The church was built to house an image of the Virgin, painted in 1409 and originally intended to be placed on the outside of a house (a common practice in Venice). Miracles (*miracoli*) began to be associated with the image in 1480, leading to a flood of votive donations that allowed the authorities to commission a church for the icon from Pietro Lombardo. One of the leading architects of his day, Lombardo created a building that relied for its effect almost entirely on color, facing his church in a variety of honey-colored marbles, porphyry panels, and serpentine inlays: legend has it that the decorations consisted of leftover materials from the Basilica. A moat-like canal enhances the effect, providing a shimmering mirror for the multi-hued marbles.

Facade detail

Interior grandeur Lombardo's innovative use of marble continues inside, which is filled with an array of sculptures that were executed in tandem with his sons, Tullio and Antonio. The best include the carving on the two pillars that support the nuns' choir (near the entrance); on the half-figures of the balustrade fronting the raised choir; among the exotica at the base of the choir's pillars. The striking ceiling is covered with 50 *Saints and Prophets* (1528), the work of Pier Pennacchi. Nicolò di Pietro's *Madonna and Child*, the miraculous image for which the church was built, adorns the high altar.

HIGHLIGHTS

- Colored marbles
- Decorative inlays
- False pillars
- Bas-reliefs
- Nuns' choir
- Balustrade
- Pillar carving
- Raised choir
- *Madonna and Child*, Nicolò de Pietro
- Ceiling

INFORMATION

- G11; Locator map D2
- Campo dei Miracoli
- 041 528 3903 or 041 275 0462
- Mon–Sat 10–5
- Campo Santa Maria Nova
- Rialto 1, 3, 82
- Good: few steps
- Inexpensive
- Santa Maria Formosa (► 44), Santi Giovanni e Paolo (► 45)

43

Santa Maria Formosa

HIGHLIGHTS

- Facades
- Martial bas-reliefs
- Plaque recording 1916 incendiary bomb
- Campanile's stone mask
- Interior
- *Madonna della Misericordia*, Bartolomeo Vivarini
- *Santa Barbara*, Palma il Vecchio

INFORMATION

- ✚ H11; Locator map E3
- ✉ Campo Santa Maria Formosa
- ☎ 041 275 0462
- 🕐 Mon–Sat 10–5
- 🍴 Campo Santa Maria Formosa
- 🚤 Rialto or Fondamente Nuove 1, 52, 82
- ♿ Good
- 💷 Inexpensive
- ↔ Piazza San Marco (➤ 38), Basilica di San Marco (➤ 41), Palazzo Ducale (➤ 42), Santa Maria dei Miracoli (➤ 43), Santi Giovanni e Paolo (➤ 45), Campo Santa Maria Formosa (➤ 57)

Santa Maria Formosa's appeal rests partly on its surrounding square. An archetypal Venetian campo, it is a pleasantly rambling affair, full of local color and lined with attractive cafés and palaces.

The structure This church takes its name from *una Madonna formosa*, a "buxom Madonna," which appeared to St. Magnus in the 7th century and instructed him to follow a small white cloud and build a church wherever it settled. The present building, completed in 1492, was grafted onto an 11th-century Byzantine church, from which it borrowed its Greek-Cross plan, a common feature of Byzantine (and later) churches dedicated to the Virgin. The facade (1542) was paid for by the Cappello family, hence its statue of Vincenzo Cappello, a Venetian admiral. Note the carved face on the bell tower to the left, one of Venice's most famous grotesques.

Interior The church's interior is a unique blend of Renaissance decoration and ersatz Byzantine cupolas, barrel vaults, and narrow-columned screens. Of particular interest are two paintings, the first being Bartolomeo Vivarini's *Madonna della Misericordia* (1473), a triptych in the first chapel on the right (south) side. It was financed by the church's congregation, depicted in the picture sheltering beneath the Virgin's protective cloak. The second, and more famous picture, Palma il Vecchio's *Santa Barbara* (1522–24), portrays the artist's daughter as its model. Barbara was martyred by her own father, who was then struck down by lightning, a death-dealing blow from the heavens that made Barbara the patron saint of artillerymen—hence the cannon at the base of the painting and the cannon-balls strewn around the chapel floor.

Santi Giovanni e Paolo

Nowhere in Venice is there a greater collection of superb sculpture under one roof than in this majestic Gothic church whose walls are lined with the funerary monuments of more than 20 of the city's doges.

Monuments Santi Giovanni e Paolo, known locally as San Zanipolo, is rivaled only by Santa Maria Gloriosa dei Frari (▶ 30). Its appeal rests on a handful of superb paintings, its tremendous tombs, and on surroundings that include the magnificent facade of the adjacent Scuola Grande di San Marco and Verrocchio's great equestrian statue of Bartolomeo Colleoni (▶ 56). The church was begun in 1246 by Doge Giacomo Tiepolo, who is buried in the most ornate of the four wall tombs built into the facade. Inside, further tombs lie ranged around the walls, many by some of Venice's finest medieval sculptors. The best include the monuments to Doge Pietro Mocenigo (*d*1476) by Pietro, Tullio, and Antonio Lombardo (left of the main door), and to Doge Michele Morosini (*d*1382), on the wall to the right of the high altar.

Paintings The most outstanding of the church's paintings are Giovanni Bellini's beautiful and recently restored polyptych of *St. Vincent Ferrer* (1464, second altar on the right) and the works in the south transept, which include *The Coronation of the Virgin*, attributed to Cima da Conegliano, and Lorenzo Lotto's wonderful *St. Antonius Pierozzi Giving Alms to the Poor* (1542).

HIGHLIGHTS

- Main portal
- *Monument to Doge Pietro Mocenigo*, Pietro Lombardo
- *St. Vincent Ferrer*, Giovanni Bellini
- Cappella della Madonna della Pace
- *St. Antonius Pierozzi Giving Alms to the Poor*, Lorenzo Lotto
- *Monument to Doge Michele Morosini*
- *Monument to Doge Andrea Vendramin* (*d*1478)
- *Monument to Doge Marco Corner* (*d*1368), Nino Pisano
- Veronese ceiling paintings, Cappella del Rosario
- *Monument to Doge Nicolò Marcello*, Pietro Lombardo

INFORMATION

- H11; Locator map E3
- Campo Santi Giovanni e Paolo
- 041 523 5913
- Mon–Sat 9–noon, 2:30–6; Sun 3–6
- Campo Santi Giovanni e Paolo
- Fondamente Nuove or Ospedale Civile 12, 13, 52
- Good: one step
- Free
- Santa Maria dei Miracoli (▶ 43)

Monument to Doge Pietro Mocenigo

San Giorgio Maggiore

HIGHLIGHTS

- Facade (1559–80)
- Lighthouses (1828)
- Campanile (1791)
- *Adoration of the Shepherds*, Jacopo Bassano
- *The Fall of Manna*, Tintoretto
- *The Last Supper*, Tintoretto
- Choir
- View from the campanile

INFORMATION

- ✚ H14; Locator map E4
- ✉ Campo San Giorgio, Isola di San Giorgio Maggiore
- ☎ 041 522 7827
- 🕐 Mon–Sat 9:30–12:30, 2:30–5; Sun 9:30–10:30, 2:30–5. Times can vary (particularly in winter)
- 🚶 Giudecca
- 🚢 San Giorgio 82
- ♿ Poor
- 🎟 Campanile inexpensive

The view from the Campanile is spell-binding, but if asked their favorite viewpoint many Venetians would probably nominate the bell tower of San Giorgio Maggiore, a magnificent Palladian church near the Giudecca.

Classical The church's dazzling marble facade provides one of the great panoramic set pieces of the Venetian skyline. Founded in 790, the first church on the site was destroyed by an earthquake in 1223, together with an adjoining Benedictine monastery built in 982. While the monastery was rebuilt in 1443, the church had to wait until 1559 and the arrival of the great Vicenzan architect, Andrea Palladio. His design for the new church adopted many of the architectural idioms of the ancient world (notably the majestic four-columned portico) to produce one of Italy's most beautiful neoclassical buildings.

Interior The ancient world also influenced the sparse interior, where light is introduced by high windows, a device borrowed from the bath-houses of 3rd-century Rome. The major works of art are Jacopo Bassano's famous *Adoration of the Shepherds* (1582), located above the second altar on the right, and a pair of outstanding paintings by Tintoretto—*The Fall of Manna* (1594) and *The Last Supper* (1594)—located on the walls of the chancel. Also worth a look is the church's choir (1594–98), tucked away behind the high altar. Few of the stalls, which depict *Scenes from the Life of St. Benedict*, have much individual delicacy, but their carving and overall effect are impressive. All else in the church pales, however, alongside the breathtaking view from the campanile, reached by an elevator at the end of the north aisle.

Carved wooden choir stalls in San Giorgio Maggiore

San Zaccaria

You'll never tire of visiting this church, a charming medley of Gothic and Renaissance architecture whose calm interior contains Giovanni Bellini's *Madonna and Child with Saints*, one of Venice's most beautiful altarpieces.

Changes San Zaccaria was founded in the 9th century, received a Romanesque veneer a century later, and was overhauled again in 1174. Rebuilding began again in the 14th century, when the church acquired a Gothic look, though no sooner had it been completed than another new church was begun. Old and new versions are still visible, the brick facade of the earlier church on the right, the white marble front of the latter to its left. The newer facade is one of the most important in Venice, displaying a moment of architectural transition from Gothic to Renaissance. The Gothic lower half is by Antonio Gambello, while the Renaissance upper section (added on Gambello's death in 1481) is the work of Mauro Coducci.

Whose who? The nave's second altar contains Giovanni Bellini's delightful *Madonna and Child with Saints* (1505). Across the nave in the second altar on the right lie the relics of San Zaccaria (Zachery or Zaccarias), the father of John the Baptist. The "museum" off the south aisle has two linked chapels, the first of which contains an early Tintoretto, *The Birth of John the Baptist* (above the main altar). Steps in the adjoining Cappella di San Tarasio lead down to a dank 9th-century crypt, final resting place of eight of the city's first doges. The chapel's vaults contain early Renaissance frescoes by Andrea del Castagno (1442), while the altars below display three Gothic altarpieces by Antonio Vivarini.

HIGHLIGHTS

- Facade bas-reliefs (1440), Antonio Gambello
- Upper facade, Mauro Coducci
- *Madonna and Child with Saints*, Giovanni Bellini
- *Tomb of Alessandro Vittoria* (1595)
- Relics of San Zaccaria
- *The Birth of John the Baptist*, Tintoretto
- Crypt
- Vault frescoes, Andrea del Castagno
- Altarpieces, Antonio Vivarini and Giovanni d'Alemagna
- Predella, Paolo Veneziano

INFORMATION

- H12; Locator map E3
- Campo di San Zaccaria
- 041 522 1257
- Daily 10–noon, 4–6
- Campo San Provolo
- San Zaccaria 1, 41, 42, 51, 52, 82
- Good
- Church free. Cappella di San Tarasio inexpensive
- Piazza San Marco (➤ 38), Basilica di San Marco (➤ 41), Palazzo Ducale (➤ 42), Scuola di San Giorgio degli Schiavoni (➤ 48), San Giovanni in Bragora (➤ 49)

Scuola di San Giorgio degli Schiavoni

HIGHLIGHTS

- Ceiling
- *St. George Slaying the Dragon*
- *Triumph of St. George*
- *St. George Baptising the Gentiles*
- *The Miracle of St. Tryphon*
- *The Agony in the Garden*
- *The Calling of St. Matthew*
- *Miracle of the Lion*
- *The Funeral of St. Jerome*
- *The Vision of St. Augustine*

INFORMATION

- J12; Locator map F3
- Calle dei Furlani
- 041 522 8828
- Apr–Oct: Tue–Sat 9:30–12:30, 3:30–6:30; Sun 9:30–12:30. Nov–Mar: Tue–Sat 10–12:30, 3–6. Sun 10–12:30
- Fondamenta di San Lorenzo
- San Zaccaria 1, 52, 82
- Good
- Moderate
- San Zaccaria (► 47), San Giovanni in Bragora (► 49), Museo Storico Navale (► 50)

Admiring paintings in galleries is enjoyable, but to look at works of art in the buildings for which they were painted is a bonus. This intimate *scuola*, with its charming Carpaccio paintings, allows you to do just that.

Slavs This tiny *scuola* (religious or charitable confraternity) was founded in 1451 to look after Venice's Dalmatian, or Slav (*Schiavoni*), population. Dalmatia, roughly present-day Croatia, was among the first territories absorbed by Venice (in the 9th century). By the 15th century the city had a large community of expatriate Dalmatian sailors, artisans, and merchants. In 1502 Carpaccio was commissioned to decorate his humble *scuola* with scenes from the lives of Dalmatia's three patron saints: George, Tryphon, and Jerome. On their completion (in 1508), the paintings were installed in the headquarters' upper gallery, only to be moved to their present position when the *scuola* was rebuilt in 1551.

Art cycle Nine paintings, plus an altarpiece by Carpaccio's son, Benedetto, lie ranged around the walls under one of the loveliest ceilings imaginable. The cycle starts on the north wall with *St. George Slaying the Dragon* (1502–08), a wonderfully graphic painting that is enlivened with a wealth of exotic and extraneous detail. Moving right you come to the *Triumph of St. George*, *St. George Baptising the Gentiles*, and *The Miracle of St. Tryphon*, which depicts the obscure boy-saint exorcising a demon from the daughter of the Roman Emperor Gordian. The next two, *The Agony in the Garden* and *The Calling of St. Matthew*, are followed by three works concerned with St. Jerome: the best known is *The Vision of St. Augustine*, in which Augustine is visited by a vision announcing Jerome's death.

San Giovanni in Bragora

Choosing a favorite small Venetian church is no easy matter as there are so many contenders, but many have a soft spot for San Giovanni in Bragora, the baptismal church of the Venetian composer Antonio Vivaldi.

Names Founded in the 8th century, San Giovanni in Bragora is one of Venice's oldest churches, its name deriving possibly from *brágora*, meaning "market-place"; or from two dialect words, *brago* ("mud") and *gora* ("stagnant canal"); or from the Greek *agora*, meaning "town square"; from *bragolare* ("to fish"); or from the region in the Middle East that yielded the relics of St. John the Baptist, to whom the church is dedicated. The Venetian composer Antonio Vivaldi was baptised here, and his original font, together with copies of the baptismal documents, stands at the beginning of the left nave.

Works of art The paintings in the lovely interior begin on the south wall to the left of the first chapel with a triptych by Francesco Bissolo and a *Madonna and Saints* by Bartolomeo Vivarini. Between these, above the confessional, stands a small Byzantine Madonna. A relief above the sacristy door is flanked on the left by Alvise Vivarini's *Risen Christ* (1498) and by Cima da Conegliano's *Constantine and St. Helena* (1502). Cima also painted the church's pictorial highlight, *The Baptism of Christ* (1494), its beautiful frame and ethereal blues offset by the high altar's stuccoed vaults. No less lovely are two paintings on the wall of the left aisle: a small *Head of the Savior* by Alvise Vivarini; and Bartolomeo Vivarini's enchanting *Madonna and Child* (1478), to the right of the second chapel.

HIGHLIGHTS

- Facade
- Vivaldi's baptismal font
- *Madonna and Saints*, Bartolomeo Vivarini
- Byzantine Madonna
- Relics of St. John the Almsgiver (second chapel on right)
- *Risen Christ*, Alvise Vivarini
- *Constantine and St. Helena*, Cima da Conegliano
- *The Baptism of Christ*, Cima da Conegliano
- *Head of the Savior*, Alvise Vivarini
- *Madonna and Child*, Bartolomeo Vivarini

INFORMATION

- J12; Locator map F3
- Campo Bandiera e Moro
- 041 522 9651
   - Mon–Fri 9:30–11, Sat 9–11, 5–7
- Campo Bandiera e Moro
- Arsenale or San Zaccaria 1, 41, 42
- Good
- Free
- San Zaccaria (▶ 47), Scuola di San Giorgio degli Schiavoni (▶ 48), Museo Storico Navale (▶ 50)

Vivaldi's baptismal font

Museo Storico Navale

- Manned torpedoes
- Painted galley friezes
- Gondola displays
- Models of Venetian galleys
- Model of the *Bucintoro*
- Padiglione delle Navi
- Painted fishing boats
- Funeral barge
- Arsenale gateway

Model of the Bucintoro

INFORMATION

- K13; Locator map F4
- Museum: Campo San Biagio. Padiglione delle Navi: Fondamenta dell'Arsenale
- 041 520 0276
- Mon–Fri 8:30–1:30; Sat 8:30–1
- Via Giuseppe Garibaldi
- Arsenale 1, 41, 42
- Poor
- Inexpensive

If you expected a dull and perfunctory museum, the Museo Storico Navale is a revelation. Its enjoyably presented displays of maritime ephemera put Venice and the sea, its inseparable ally, into a clear historical context.

Boats The idea of a maritime museum originated in 1815 with the Austrians, who collected remnants of the Venetian Navy (dispersed and partly destroyed by Napoleon) and mixed them with scale models of Venetian vessels and other pieces of maritime ephemera. In 1958 the collection, swollen over the years, was moved to its present site close to the entrance to the Arsenale, the great shipyards that once produced the galleys that formed the cornerstone of Venice's far-flung empire. Before or after seeing the museum, it is well worth walking the short distance north to Campo Arsenale to admire the fine Renaissance gateway (1460), which marks the entrance to the yards (now in the hands of the Italian Navy).

Maritime collection The four-story museum traces the history of the Venetian and Italian navies, illustrating their development with a succession of uniforms, medals, flags, pendants, maps, diagrams, cannon, mortars, machine-guns, and beautifully crafted scale models of forts and boats. Look for the models of the *triremi*, the oar-driven galleys that formed the core of the Venetian fleet. Displays on the fourth floor are devoted to the gondola. The mezzanine has a shimmering collection of shells and an exhibit about the unexpectedly close links between the maritime traditions of Venice and Sweden. Be sure to visit the separate Padiglione delle Navi, a wonderful collection of gondolas, funeral barques, and other lovely old boats housed in the Arsenale's former oarsmakers' sheds.

VENICE's
best

51

Paintings

The Miracle of the Cross at Ponte San Lorenzo by Gentile Bellini

GENTILE BELLINI
The Miracle of the Cross at Ponte San Lorenzo (1500)
One of a cycle of paintings depicting "The Miracles of the True Cross," this picture shows the head of the Scuola di San Giovanni Evangelista holding aloft a reliquary containing a fragment of the "True Cross" (the reliquary had accidentally been dropped into a canal and floated miraculously to the surface).
Location Gallerie dell'Accademia (▶ 33)

GIOVANNI BELLINI
Madonna and Child between Sts. Nicholas, Peter, Mark, and Benedict (1488)
The effect of this painting is enhanced by the perspective used to place the Madonna in her gold-lined recess, and the manner in which the frame is designed to continue the painting's perspective scheme. The picture was a gift from noblemen Pietro (Peter) Pesaro and his sons Niccolò, Marco, and Benedetto—hence the choice of saints depicted.
Location Santa Maria Gloriosa dei Frari (▶ 30)

VITTORE CARPACCIO
St. George Slaying the Dragon (1502–08)
Note the remains of the dragon's earlier victims, depicted in grisly detail in the foreground of the painting, and the manner in which the saint's lance divides the picture into compositional "triangles." Each section has its own color and narrative preoccupation: dragon and city, St. George and Selene (the princess he has saved), the sky, and the human debris of the foreground.
Location Scuola di San Giorgio degli Schiavoni (▶ 48)

VITTORE CARPACCIO
Two Women (1507)
This picture was long thought to depict a pair of courtesans, though the distinctive hairstyles and plunging necklines of the dresses were typical of many women of the time.
Location Museo Civico Corter (▶ 39)

GIAN ANTONIO FUMIANI
The Miracles and Martyrdom of St. Pantaleone (1704)
Although not artistically distinguished, this ceiling painting impresses by its sheer scale, its 60 linked panels forming the world's largest area of painted canvas.
Location San Pantalon (▶ 55)

FAMILY PORTRAIT

Iacopo Pesaro, who commissioned Titian's *Madonna di Ca' Pesaro*, is depicted in the painting in front of the knight on the left (who may be a self-portrait of Titian). Pesaro led a fleet against the Turks in 1502, partly in response to a call from the Borgia pope, Alexander VI—hence the knight in armor behind Pesaro, whose standard bears the Pesaro and Borgia coats of arms. The same figure leads a turbanned Turk and black slave toward St. Peter, a symbol of their conversion and of the Christian spirit of the campaign. On the right, St. Francis holds his hands over Iacopo's brother, Francesco, while the boy looking out from the painting is Iacopo's nephew and heir, Lunardo. The face of the Madonna was modeled on Titian's wife, Celia, who died soon after in childbirth.

JACOPO ROBUSTI TINTORETTO

Paradiso (1588–92)

At 1,500 square feet this is the world's largest single oil painting. Painted free for the state when Tintoretto was in his seventies, it depicts the regiment of the saved as described in Canto XXX of Dante's *Paradiso*.

Location Palazzo Ducale (➤ 42)

JACOPO ROBUSTI TINTORETTO

Crucifixion (1565)

Victorian critic John Ruskin wrote of this painting: "I must leave this picture to work its will on the spectator, for it is beyond all analysis and above all praise." Novelist Henry James thought: "Surely no single picture in the world contains more of human life…there is everything in it."

Location Scuola Grande di San Rocco (➤ 29)

TIZIANO VECELLIO (TITIAN)

Assumption (1516–18)

This powerful painting sits above the Frari's high altar, and is designed to attract your attention from most parts of the church. It was not always highly esteemed, having been criticized as too revolutionary by the Franciscans who commissioned it, and was kept in storage until the beginning of the 20th century.

Location Santa Maria Gloriosa dei Frari (➤ 30)

TIZIANO VECELLIO (TITIAN)

Madonna di Ca' Pesaro (1526)

Bishop Pesaro (see panel) lies buried in a tomb to the right of the painting commissioned in 1519. Note the two columns that bisect the picture and the off-center position of the Madonna, both interesting compositional devices.

Location Santa Maria Gloriosa dei Frari (➤ 30)

PAOLO VERONESE

Supper in the House of Levi (1573)

This picture was painted as a *Last Supper* for the refectory of Santi Giovanni e Paolo, but after complaints from the Inquisition—who objected to its "buffoons, drunkards, Germans, dwarfs and similar indecencies"—Veronese changed its name (but not its content). Veronese himself is the figure in green, center left.

Location Gallerie dell'Accademia (➤ 33)

Carpaccio's Two Women

ST. URSULA

Carpaccio's painting cycle in the Accademia tells the story of St. Ursula, daughter of the Breton King Maurus, and her proposed marriage to Hereus, son of the English King Conon. It was agreed that the ceremony would take place on two conditions: first, that Hereus wait three years, and second that he convert to Christianity and accompany Ursula on a pilgrimage to Rome. Neither demand seemed unreasonable, except that the pilgrimage was to be made in the company of "11,000 virgins," and that the whole party were eventually massacred at Cologne on their return from Rome.

Carpaccio's St. George Slaying the Dragon

Churches

In the Top 25

SEE ALSO LISTINGS (➤ 26–50)

Gesuiti trompe-l'oeil

ARCHWAY

Not far from San Giacomo, *en route* for Santa Maria Gloriosa dei Frari, stands the Scuola Grande di San Giovanni Evangelista. Once among the city's richest *scuole*, it was responsible, among other things, for commissioning the great *Miracles of the True Cross* cycle now in the Accademia (➤ 33). Today, its buildings are mostly given over to conferences and are closed to the public. Anyone, however, can enjoy its stunning archway, designed by Pietro Lombardo in 1481. The eagle in the lunette is the symbol of St. John (San Giovanni).

GESUITI

This large, dank church, built by the Jesuits in 1715, is renowned for its extraordinary marble *trompe-l'œil*, best seen in the pulpit on the left, whose solid stone is carved to resemble pelmets, tassels, and curtains. The church also boasts Titian's *Martyrdom of St. Lawrence* (first chapel on the left) and Tintoretto's *Assumption of the Virgin* (left transept).

➕ G10–H10 ✉ Campo dei Gesuiti ☎ 041 528 6579 🕐 Daily 10–noon, 5–7 🚤 Fondamente Nuove 41, 42, 51, 52 ♿ Good 🎫 Free

SAN FRANCESCO DELLA VIGNA

San Francesco takes its name from a vineyard (*vigna*) left to the Franciscans here in 1253. Many alterations have been made since, not least the facade, built by Palladio between 1562 and 1572. Despite its shabby surroundings, the church has many fine tombs, marble reliefs by Pietro Lombardo, a delightful cloister, and several good paintings, the best being Antonio da Negroponte's *Madonna and Child* (1450), on the right-hand wall of the right transept.

➕ J11 ✉ Campo della Confraternità ☎ 041 520 6102 🕐 Daily 7–noon, 3–7 🚤 San Zaccaria or Celestia 41, 42, 51, 52 ♿ Good 🎫 Free

SAN GIACOMO DELL'ORIO

Few Venetian buildings feel as old as San Giacomo, founded in the 9th century and added to over the years to produce a pleasing architectural hybrid. The 14th-century Gothic ship's-keel ceiling is outstanding, as is the wooden Tuscan statue of the *Madonna and Child*. There are magnificent paintings in the old and new sacristies (some by Veronese), two ancient marble pillars in the nave (stolen during the Fourth Crusade), a *Crucifix* by Lorenzo Veneziano, and a high altarpiece by Lorenzo Lotto of the *Madonna and Child* (1546).

➕ E10 ✉ Campo San Giacomo dell'Orio ☎ 041 524 0672 🕐 Mon–Sat 10–5 🚤 Riva di Biasio or San Stae 1 ♿ Good 🎫 Inexpensive

SAN GIOBBE

San Giobbe began life as a 13th-century chapel dedicated to Job (Giobbe), a figure invoked against the plague. The fine portal and its four saints (1471) are the work of Pietro Lombardo. The interior is known for the Cappella Martini, created for expatriate silk weavers from

Campanile, San Francesco della Vigna

Lucca—hence the majolica work by the Tuscan-based della Robbia family. The lions in the right aisle decorate the tomb of a 17th-century French ambassador. The sacristy off the right nave has a lovely ceiling and a fine triptych by Antonio Vivarini.

✚ D9 ✉ Campo San Giobbe ☎ 041 524 1889 🕓 Mon–Sat 10–noon, 4–6 🚤 Ponte dei Tre Archi 41, 42, 51, 52 ♿ Good 🎫 Free

SANTA MARIA DEL GIGLIO

This church takes its alternative name (Santa Maria Zobenigo) from the Jubanico family, who reputedly financed its building in the 9th century. Another family, the 17th-century Barbaro clan, commissioned the present facade. Its five statues represent five of the Barbaro brothers, while the martial reliefs depict fortresses that featured in the brothers' military careers. Inside, the high altar is adorned with works by Tintoretto, although the church's highlight is its lovingly displayed collection of saints' relics.

✚ F13 ✉ Campo Santa Maria Zobenigo ☎ 041 522 5739 or 041 275 0462 🕓 Mon–Sat 10–5 🚤 Santa Maria del Giglio 1 ♿ Poor (steps inside church) 🎫 Inexpensive

SAN NICOLÒ DEI MENDICOLI

San Nicolò is one of Venice's oldest and most charming churches. It was built in the 12th century, and since 1966 has been restored by the Venice in Peril Fund. The interior is beautifully decorated with marbles, statues, paintings, and fine gilded woodwork.

✚ B12–C12 ✉ Campo San Nicolò ☎ 041 528 5952 🕓 Mon–Sat 10–noon, 4–5:30; Sun 4–6 🚤 San Basilio 82 ♿ Good 🎫 Free

SAN PANTALON

San Pantalon is best known for its gargantuan ceiling painting, Gian Antonio Fumiani's *The Miracles and Martyrdom of St. Pantaleone* (1704). Smaller paintings include Veronese's *St. Pantaleone Healing a Boy* (1587; second chapel on the right) and the *Coronation of the Virgin* (1444) by Antonio Vivarini and Giovanni d'Alemagna (chapel to the left as you face the chancel).

✚ D12 ✉ Campo San Pantalon 🕓 Daily 8–11:30, 3:30–7; Sat 4:30–7 🚤 San Tomà 1, 82 ♿ Good 🎫 Free

SAN POLO

Founded in 837 but much altered since, the church of San Polo is renowned for Giandomenico Tiepolo's *Via Crucis*, or *Stations of the Cross* (1747), an 18-panel cycle of paintings in the sacristy. Tintoretto's turbulent *Last Supper* (1547) hangs to the sacristy's left (on the west wall), while the apse chapel to the left of the high altar contains Veronese's *Marriage of the Virgin*.

✚ E12–F11 ✉ Campo San Polo ☎ 041 523 7631 or 041 275 0462 🕓 Mon–Sat 10–5 🚤 San Silvestro 1 ♿ Good 🎫 Inexpensive

MINOR CHURCHES

During your exploration of the city look for the following:

● Gesuati—notable for its richly decorated interior, ceiling fresco by G.B. Tiepolo and paintings by Tintoretto, Piazzetta, and Sebastiano Ricci (✚ E13).

● San Giacomo di Rialto—a tiny 5th-century church, reputedly Venice's oldest, known for its Gothic portico and lovely clock (✚ G11).

● San Moisè—with the most elaborate baroque facade in the city; look for the many grotesques (✚ G12).

● San Salvatore—with a beautiful Renaissance interior and two paintings by Titian: *The Annunciation* (third altar on the right) and *The Transfiguration* above the high altar (✚ G11).

● San Trovaso—containing Tintoretto's final two works (either side of the choir) and the superb *St. Chrysogonus on Horseback* (chapel left as you face the high altar) by Michele Giambono (✚ E13).

San Nicolò dei Mendicoli

Squares

In the Top 25
🔟 PIAZZA SAN MARCO (► 38)

BARTOLOMEO COLLEONI

Born in Bergamo, Colleoni, the noted 15th-century mercenary, began his military career in Naples aged 19, entering Venetian service in 1431. After spells working for Milan, he returned to the Venetian cause in 1455. Over the next 20 years, however, he was called upon to fight only once. His name is a corruption of *coglioni*, meaning "testicles," a play on words of which Colleoni was proud (*coglioni* featured conspicuously on his emblem). Thomas Coryat, an English traveler to Venice in 1611, repeated a story (put about by Colleoni himself) that "Bathelmew Coleon…had his name from having *three* stones, for the Italian word Coglione doth signifie a testicle."

CAMPO DEI MORI

This sleepy little square may take its name either from the Moorish merchants who traded in the *fondaco* nearby, or from three silk merchants—Robia, Sandi, and Alfani Mastelli—who left the Peloponnese (Morea) in 1112 to settle in the Palazzo Mastelli north of the *campo* (recognizable by the bas-relief of a camel). In time they may have inspired the so-called *Mori* (Moors), three statues built into the walls of the piazza's houses. The building just east of the square at No. 3399 (with a plaque) was home to the painter Tintoretto between 1574 and his death in 1594.

➕ F9   ✉ Cannaregio   🚊 Madonna dell'Orto 41, 42, 51, 52

CAMPO SANTI GIOVANNI E PAOLO

The church of Santi Giovanni e Paolo in this square should not distract you from the statue of Bartolomeo Colleoni at its center, nor the lovely facade of the Scuola Grande di San Marco on its northern flank. The *scuola*, now a hospital, was once the wealthiest in Venice and boasted a headquarters that was rivaled only by the Scuola Grande di San Rocco (► 29). Its facade was begun in 1487 by Pietro Lombardo (responsible for many of the sculptures in the church) and completed eight years later by Mauro Coducci, an architect active in the nearby churches of Santa Maria Formosa and San Zaccaria (► 44 and 47). The statue of Colleoni (1481–96), often called Italy's greatest equestrian sculpture, is mostly the work of the Florentine sculptor Andrea Verrocchio. Colleoni was a famous *condottiere*, or mercenary soldier (see panel), who left his vast fortune to Venice on the condition that the city erected a statue of him in Piazza San Marco. The state took his money, but was unwilling to glorify any individual in its most famous square and so slyly erected a statue in the more modest *Campo* San Marco instead.

➕ H11   ✉ Castello   🍴 Cafés   🚊 Ospedale Civile 52

CAMPO SANTA MARGHERITA

This may well become your favorite Venetian square, thanks mainly to its friendly and informal air, its collection of pleasant little bars and cafés, and its easy-going streetlife, which reminds you that Venice is still—just—a living city. Venetians meet here to chat, shop, and sip coffee while their children play raucously on the square's ancient flagstones.

Piazza San Marco

Causin (► 76), noted for its ice cream, is the longest established of the cafés, but Il Caffè and Il Doge are both equally fine places to sit and watch the world go by. The square is convenient to many sights, notably San Pantalon (► 55), the Scuola Grande dei Carmini (► 28), San Sebastiano (► 27), the Scuola Grande di San Rocco and Frari (► 29 and 30), the Accademia (► 33), and the Ca' Rezzonico (► 31).

🔲 D12 ⊠ Dorsoduro 🍴 Cafés 🚤 Ca' Rezzonico 1

CAMPO SANTA MARIA FORMOSA

Like all of Venice's more intriguing squares, Campo Santa Maria Formosa is distinguished by an old-world Venetian charm, assured by a combination of market stalls, local streetlife, and welcoming cafés and bars. Although only a stone's throw from Piazza San Marco, the square escapes the attention of most tourists but is convenient to several key sights, not least of which is the church of Santa Maria Formosa, whose crumbling facade dominates its southern flank (► 44).

🔲 H11 ⊠ Castello 🍴 Cafés 🚤 Rialto 1, 82

Campo Santa Margherita

CAMPO SAN POLO

Campo San Polo is the largest of Venice's squares after Piazza San Marco, but sits at the heart of the smallest of the city's six *sestieri*. Once the scene of bullfights, mass sermons, and masked balls, it is now a homey place for elderly matrons and their dogs, and groups of mothers with their children, who play soccer and ride their bikes. Informal sidewalk cafés provide a vantage point on the comings and goings, while the church of San Polo (► 55) and the Palazzo Soranzo (once home to Casanova) add a more formal note to the square.

🔲 E11–F11 ⊠ San Polo 🍴 Cafés 🚤 San Silvestro 1

CAMPO SANTO STEFANO (CAMPO FRANCESCO MOROSINI)

After Campo Santa Margherita, this is probably the most pleasant square for a break from sightseeing, and in particular from the church of Santo Stefano (► 32) and the nearby Accademia (► 33). Until 1802 it was used for bullfights, during which bulls or oxen were tied to a stake and baited by dogs. For years the area was grassy, all except for a stone avenue known as the Liston. This became such a popular place to stroll that it led to a Venetian expression *andare al liston*, meaning "to go for a walk." The square's nicest café is Paolin, considered by many to serve the best ice cream in the city.

🔲 F12 ⊠ San Marco 🍴 Cafés 🚤 San Samuele 82

SIOR ANTONIO

A fourth figure complements Campo dei Mori's three famous Moorish statues. Known as Sior Antonio Rioba, and distinguished by its rusty metal nose, it peers down from the corner of a building on the east of the square. Anonymous denunciations of the state were once signed with his name and left pinned at his feet, a practice recalling "Pasqualino" in Rome, a statue at which *pasquinades* (usually papal denunciations) were left.

Views

View from the Campanile

PEOPLE-WATCHING

The Loggia dei Cavalli is home to the famous bronze horses of the Basilica di San Marco (though today's versions are copies, the originals are kept inside the Basilica to protect them from pollution), but it also has a tremendous view over Piazza San Marco and its swirling crowds. There are few better places in the whole of Italy to indulge in people-watching.

➕ G12–H12 ✉ Piazza San Marco ☎ 041 522 5205 🕐 Mon–Fri 9:30–5:30; Sun 1–5:30 🍴 Piazza San Marco 🚤 Vallaresso or San Zaccaria 1, 3, 4, 52, 82 ♿ Poor 🎟 Inexpensive

CAMPANILE

You will probably face lines for the Campanile (➤ 40), but the view—which extends to the Alps on a clear day—is more than worth the wait. Goethe first saw the sea from here, while Galileo used the panorama to demonstrate his telescope.

➕ G12 ✉ Piazza San Marco ☎ 041 522 4064 🕐 Jul–Aug: 9:30–7:30. Rest of year: 9:30 to between 3:30 and 7 🍴 Piazza San Marco 🚤 Vallaresso or San Zaccaria 1, 3, 4, 52, 82 ♿ Poor 🎟 Moderate

PONTE DELL'ACCADEMIA

All the bridges across the Grand Canal (➤ 26) have mesmerizing views, but none perhaps as pretty as those from the Ponte dell'Accademia. Below you boats and gondolas flit about, while the Grand Canal curves gently to the east and west, with views of distant palaces and the church of Santa Maria della Salute (➤ 36).

➕ E13 ✉ Canal Grande 🚤 Accademia 1, 82 ♿ Poor 🎟 Free

PONTE DI RIALTO

While the Ponte dell'Accademia has a sublime general view of the Grand Canal, the Ponte di Rialto provides an overview of a stretch that is narrow yet frantically busy. You could spend a lot of time here simply soaking in the comings and goings beneath you, or casting your eye over the people jostling for position on the Fondamenta del Vin.

➕ G11 ✉ Canal Grande 🍴 Cafés on the Fondamenta del Vin 🚤 Rialto 1, 82 ♿ Poor 🎟 Free

PUNTA DELLA DOGANA

The *sestiere* of Dorsoduro narrows to a point at the Punta della Dogana to give a fine view across the mouth of the Grand Canal to the north (taking in the Campanile and Palazzo Ducale) and across the Canale della Giudecca to the south (with excellent views of San Giorgio Maggiore and the Giudecca).

➕ G13 ✉ Canal Grande 🚤 Santa Maria della Salute 1 ♿ Good 🎟 Free

SAN GIORGIO MAGGIORE

The view from the bell tower of Palladio's church is perhaps the best in the city, surpassing that of the Campanile by virtue of the fact that it has a panorama that includes the Campanile and gives a better overview of the lagoon and the Giudecca.

➕ H14 ✉ Campo San Giorgio, Isola di San Giorgio Maggiore ☎ 041 522 7827 🕐 Mon–Sat 9:30–12:30, 2:30–5; Sun 9:30–10:30, 2:30–5. Check as times can vary (particularly in winter). 🍴 Giudecca 🚤 San Giorgio 82 ♿ Poor 🎟 Inexpensive

Facades

CA' PESARO

Like many of Venice's finest palaces, the Ca' Pesaro presents its best face to the Grand Canal, but with some judicious route-finding its waterfront facade can also be glimpsed from the ends of several alleys off the Strada Nova. It was bought as three separate buildings in 1628 by the Pesaro family, who subsequently commissioned Baldassare Longhena, one of Venice's leading 17th-century architects, to unite the component parts behind one of the city's grandest baroque facades. Today it houses Venice's Museo Orientale, a collection of Chinese and Japanese art and artifacts.

✚ F10 ✉ Canal Grande-Fondamenta Pesaro ☎ Museo Orientale 041 524 1173 ◷ Museo Orientale Tue–Sun 9–2 🚤 San Stae 1 ♿ Poor 🖐 Museo Orientale moderate

PALAZZO DARIO

The Palazzo Dario possesses perhaps the most charming facade of any Venetian palace, its appeal heightened by the building's rather alarming lean. Built in the 1480s, it was probably designed by Pietro Lombardo, whose use of inlaid colored marbles is repeated in his masterpiece, Santa Maria dei Miracoli (➤ 43). It has long been believed that the palace is cursed. It is best seen from the Grand Canal or the Santa Maria del Giglio landing stage opposite.

✚ F13 ✉ Calle Barbaro ◷ Not open to the public 🚤 Santa Maria del Giglio 1

PALAZZO VENDRAMIN-CALERGI

The masterpiece of the Grand Canal, this palace was begun by Mauro Coducci at the end of the 15th century and finished in the first decade of the 16th century, probably by Tullio Lombardo. The composer Richard Wagner occupied a 15-room suite here during his last months. When he died in the palace in February 1883, his body was taken to the station by gondola in the dead of night for subsequent burial at Bayreuth. Today, the palace is the winter home of the Casinò Municipale. The facade is best seen from the Canal or from the Calle del Megio opposite.

✚ F10 ✉ Canal Grande-Calle Larga Vendramin 🚤 San Marcuola 1, 82

FACADES

A palace's waterfront facade was the most elaborate and the only one faced with stone, which was both costlier and heavier than brick, and therefore a burden on the building's foundations (these consisted of wooden piles driven into the mud). The first floor was marked by a gate opening onto the canal and entrance hall (*andron*), used for deliveries and access by gondola. Above, windows mark the *mezzanino*, a labyrinth of small rooms used as offices, and above them a row of larger windows which indicate the *piano nobile*, the grandest of the palace's living areas. This consisted of suites arranged around the *portego*, a broad corridor through the building that encouraged cool breezes to pass through in summer.

Facade of the Palazzo Dario

Boat Trips

Vaporetto on the Grand Canal

In the Top 25

1 CANAL GRANDE (➤ 26)

ISLANDS

The No. 12 *vaporetto* from the Fondamente Nuove runs every 60 to 90 minutes to the islands of Burano and Torcello, a 45-minute trip that provides not only two interesting end destinations, but also gives excellent views of Venice and the Venetian lagoon. (Panel ➤ 7 for details of the special one-day boat pass to the islands.)

H10 Fondamente Nuove Fondamente Nuove 12 Expensive

LA GIUDECCA AND THE DOCKS

Catching *vaporetto* 82 at San Zaccaria and staying on board past San Giorgio and the Giudecca to Piazzale Roma will give you not only a good view of San Giorgio Maggiore and the Giudecca ahead (and San Marco behind), but also an interesting insight into the area around the docks and Stazione Marittima, the busy and little-visited commercial port area in the southeast of the city.

H12 Riva degli Schiavoni San Zaccaria 82 Moderate

LIDO

In the late 19th century the Lido—which lies 20 minutes south of Venice by boat—was one of the most exclusive swimming establishments in Europe. This is less true today and, unless you wish to spend time on a beach during your stay, the island is best seen from the No. 1 *vaporetto*, which can be boarded at any of the stops on the Grand Canal or San Zaccaria. The service provides fine views back to San Marco and a view of enough of the Lido to satisfy most people's curiosity.

H12 Riva degli Schiavoni San Zaccaria 1 Moderate

MURANO AND ARSENALE

The Arsenale, Venice's vast former shipyards, are now occupied by the military and are out of bounds to the general public. The only way to catch a glimpse of the yards, whose boats provided the wherewithal for Venice's supremacy at sea, is to take one of the *motoscafi* (41, 42, 51, 52) that ply the waters off the northern edge of the Arsenale. Note that the 42 continues to Murano, circles the island, and then returns to the Fondamente Nuove before proceeding around the northern shore of the city to the Canale di Cannaregio and Piazzale Roma.

K12–K13 Campiello della Malvasia Tana 42 Moderate

GONDOLA RIDES

Hiring a gondola is enchanting but expensive. In theory, the official tariff is around 62 euros; L120,000 for a 50-minute ride for up to five passengers, rising to about 77 euros; L150,000 for the same trip between 8PM and 8AM. An extra 36 euros; L70,000 is levied for each additional 25 minutes, and more for any musical accompaniment. In practice, rates are more negotiable, so confirm the rate and duration before departure. Do not be afraid to walk away or haggle if the prices seem too high–there are plenty of gondoliers. Most gondoliers have a set route, so if you wish to see a particular part of the city discuss your preferences before striking a deal. Note the location of official stands: Riva del Carbon (near the Rialto); Campo San Moisè; Santa Maria del Giglio; Bacino Orseolo (northwest of Piazza San Marco); at the train station; and the Danieli hotel.

What's Free

CHURCHES

Churches rarely charge, and where they do, as in the case of the Frari (➤ 30), the entrance fee is invariably modest. Most have some artistic treasure—a sculpture, a Tintoretto, a Bellini altarpiece—which makes a visit more than worthwhile (➤ 52–53 and 54–55).

MUSIC

You may occasionally come across free organ, choral, or chamber recitals in Venetian churches. Look for posters or contact the tourist office for details. Mass is usually sung in the Basilica di San Marco at 9AM on weekdays and 10AM on Sundays and feast days. Vespers are sung at 5:30PM in winter and 6PM in summer.

PAINTINGS

Many of Venice's finest paintings can be seen for free. These include masterpieces by Veronese (➤ 27), Tintoretto (➤ 35), Titian (➤ 53), and the Bellini altarpieces of San Pietro Martire, Santi Giovanni e Paolo, and San Zaccaria (➤ 20, 45, and 47).

RIALTO MARKETS

The Rialto has it all, whether you want to shop for souvenirs, people-watch, or revel in the sights and smells of a market. Early in the morning, before the crowds arrive, is the best time for a stroll around the fantastic medley of food and fish stalls (➤ 83).

SQUARES

Venetian squares offer the chance not only to watch your fellow visitors, but also provide an opportunity to take in the Venetians at work and play. Most squares have a variety of cafés with outside tables. For the price of a cup of coffee you can observe everything from the comfort of a café terrace (➤ 56–57).

STROLLING

Venice's finest free sight is Venice itself. No city in the world has as many beautiful views, intriguing streets, and magical buildings. Almost any walk has its rewards, the more so if you stroll around early in the morning or late at night (➤ 22–24).

PARKS AND GARDENS

Venice is a city whose peculiar make-up means it has little room left over for public parks and gardens. Still, there are one or two areas of green space. In the heart of the city these are restricted to the small Giardinetti Reali (✚ G12–G13) immediately south of Piazza San Marco (but entered from the waterfront). On the city's fringes are the much larger Giardini Pubblici (✚ L14) and more modest Giardino Papadopoli (✚ C11–D11). Further afield, the islands of Burano and Torcello have extensive areas of open space (➤ 22–23).

Giardini Pubblici

For Kids

RESTAURANTS

Pizzerias and more casual restaurants are usually welcoming, though special facilities such as high chairs are rarely available. If you want a small serving ask for *una mezza porzione*. Upscale restaurants on the whole do not take kindly to smaller children, though the Italians are generally far more tolerant than many northern Europeans.

Carnival masks

BOAT TRIPS

Children should be captivated by the things to see from Venice's *vaporetti* and *motoscafi*. The best short trip is along the Grand Canal (▶ 26), while the best longer ride (on a larger boat) is out to the islands of Burano, Murano, and Torcello (▶ 20–21).

GLASS-BLOWING

Many of the glass workshops and showrooms on Murano (▶ 19) provide the chance to watch glass-blowers in action (glass-blowers can usually be persuaded to make a small glass gift for children).

GONDOLAS

Gondolas are large enough to accommodate at least two adults and two children, and are rented by time rather than the number of passengers. See panel (▶ 60) for details of prices and how to hire gondolas. Note that Grand Canal rides can be choppy.

ICE CREAM

Italian ice cream should satisfy the most demanding of young palates. Some of Venice's best *gelato* is to be found at Paolin in Campo Santo Stefano (Campo Francesco Morosini), Causin in Campo Santa Margherita, and Nico on the Zattere ai Gesuati (▶ 76–77 for more details).

LIDO

The Lido offers the chance to swim or play on the beach, as well as the excitement of the boat trip from Venice (take *vaporetto* No. 1). It is also possible to rent bikes and pedal boats at several outlets along the promenade. Note that many of the Lido's beaches are owned by hotels; public beaches (*spiaggia* or *zona comunale*) are clearly marked.

MARKETS

The strange sights, sounds, and smells of the Rialto markets (▶ 83) are memorable, although the more bizarre and bloody seafood of the Pescheria (fish market) may upset the younger ones.

MASKS

Children might enjoy buying and wearing Venice's famous masks, or simply window-shopping among the city's better-known mask shops (▶ 80–81).

MUSEUMS

Of Venice's museums the maritime theme at the Museo Storico Navale (▶ 50) should appeal to children, and the Museo Civico Correr (▶ 39) has an interesting, costume, and weaponry section.

VENICE
where to

Luxury Hotels

PRICES

Expect to pay for a double room per night:

Luxury	over 258 euros; L500,000
Expensive	129–258 euros; L250–500,000
Mid-range	77–155 euros; L150–300,000
Budget	under 88 euros; L170,000;

Italy's hotels, including those in Venice, are classified by the state system into five categories, from one star (basic) to five stars (luxury). The prices of individual rooms should be displayed in the lobby and in the room itself. Prices for different rooms often vary within a hotel, so if a room is too expensive be sure to ask if another is available for less (you may well be shown the most expensive room first). Watch out for supplements for breakfast, which may be charged even if you do not take it, and in peak periods remember that hotels may insist that you take half- or full board.

CIPRIANI ★★★★

Venice's most expensive hotel is a relative newcomer, having opened in 1963, but has quickly become a byword for luxury. Facilities include a Jacuzzi in every suite, an Olympic-sized swimming-pool, butler service, and a renowned restaurant. The location in gardens on the eastern end of the Giudecca is away from the tourist hustle, but can make you feel slightly isolated from the city. Virtually all 104 rooms (50 suites) have superb views.

✚ H14 ✉ Giudecca 10 ☎ 041 520 7744; fax 041 520 3930 🚤 Zitelle 52, 82 ❓ Private launch service

DANIELI ★★★★★

A hotel since 1822, the Danieli is the choice of visiting royalty and other VIPs. It ranks as the finest of Venice's luxury hotels—but stay in the old wing of the Gothic *palazzo* rather than the newer annexe built in 1948. 230 rooms (11 suites).

✚ H12 ✉ Riva degli Schiavoni-Calle delle Rasse, Castello 4196 ☎ 041 522 6480; fax 041 520 0208 🚤 San Zaccaria 1, 82

EUROPA E REGINA ★★★★★

Venice's "Big Three"—the Gritti, Cipriani, and Danieli—tend to overshadow this CIGA-owned hotel, but its prices are some of the most reasonable of the city's luxury hotels. Most of the 192 rooms are spacious and many enjoy glorious views over a courtyard garden or across the Grand Canal, while the restaurant's canal terrace and garden are wonderfully evocative places to dine.

✚ G13 ✉ Calle Larga (Viale) XXII Marzo, San Marco 2159 ☎ 041 520 0477; fax 041 523 1533 🚤 Vallaresso or Santa Maria del Giglio 1, 82

GRITTI PALACE ★★★★★

Not the most expensive hotel in Venice, but—along with the Danieli—the one traditionally considered to have the most class and *élan*. Greta Garbo and Winston Churchill are among its past guests. Housed in a 15th-century *palazzo* close to the Grand Canal, its 93 rooms and reception areas are all impeccably grand, as is the service. Rooms vary considerably from small singles to enormous suites. A private launch and private beach are both available.

✚ F13 ✉ Santa Maria del Giglio, San Marco 2467 ☎ 041 794611; fax 041 520 0942 🚤 Santa Maria del Giglio 1

MONACO AND GRAND CANAL ★★★★

Not as famous as other hotels in its class, but almost as stylish and elegant. As its name suggests, it overlooks the Grand Canal, and the nicest of the 70 rooms enjoy views across to Santa Maria della Salute. Excellent restaurant and breakfast terrace.

✚ G13 ✉ Calle Vallaresso, San Marco 1325 ☎ 041 520 0211; fax 041 520 0501 🚤 Vallaresso 1, 82

Expensive Hotels

ACCADEMIA-VILLA MARAVEGE ★★★

A 17th-century *palazzo* just west of the Accademia that once housed the Russian Embassy. Its popular 27 rooms are still grand and are furnished with antiques, although some are rather small. There is a garden with a Grand Canal view.

✚ E13 ✉ Fondamenta Bollani, Dorsoduro 1058 ☎ 041 521 0188; fax 041 523 9152 🚤 Accademia 1, 82

CAVALLETTO E DOGE ★★★★

This 95-room hotel north of Piazza San Marco has been in business for over 200 years. Good restaurant, light and airy rooms.

✚ G12 ✉ Calle Cavalletto, San Marco 1107 ☎ 041 520 0955; fax 041 523 8184 🚤 Vallaresso 1, 82

GIORGIONE ★★★★

A 68-room hotel with modern facilities; one of the best in the category. Rooms are in period style, with elegant fabrics and fine attention to detail.

✚ G10 ✉ Campo Santi Apostoli, Cannaregio 4587 ☎ 041 522 5810; fax 041 523 9092 🚤 Ca' d'Oro 1

METROPOLE ★★★★

Elegant and sophisticated hotel with 72 rooms on the busy waterfront by the church of the Pietà. Rooms are spacious and romantic, with antiques, paintings, and period furniture; some have broad lagoon views and others look onto the canal and gardens.

✚ J12 ✉ Riva degli Schiavoni 4149, Castello ☎ 041 520 5044; fax 041 522 3679 🚤 Vallaresso 1, 3, 4, 82

SAN MOISÈ ★★★

The 16 rooms in this tranquil but centrally located hotel vary in size. All are furnished with Murano glass lamps, old mirrors, and other antique touches.

✚ F12 ✉ Piscina San Moisè, San Marco 2058 ☎ 041 520 3755; fax 041 521 0670 🚤 Vallaresso or Santa Maria del Giglio 1, 82

SATURNIA & INTERNAZIONALE ★★★★

Romantic, old-fashioned hotel in a peaceful setting. All 95 rooms differ slightly, the best look on to the courtyard garden. Excellent restaurant.

✚ F12–13 ✉ Calle Larga (Viale) XXII Marzo, San Marco 2398 ☎ 041 520 8377; fax 041 520 5858 or 041 520 7131 🚤 Santa Maria del Giglio 1

SCANDINAVIA ★★★

There is considerable variety in the 27 rooms of this fine hotel, but all are comfortable and spacious. Good location on one of Venice's nicest squares.

✚ H11 ✉ Campo Santa Maria Formosa, Castello 5240 ☎ 041 522 3507; fax 041 523 5232 🚤 Rialto 1, 82

STURION ★★★

The best of this welcoming hotel's 11 rooms—which vary in price—look over the Grand Canal. Some non-smoking rooms.

✚ F11 ✉ Calle del Storione, San Polo 679 ☎ 041 523 6243; fax 041 522 8378 🚤 San Silvestro 1

TIGHT SQUEEZE

Venice has been accommodating visitors for hundreds of years, although over the last couple of decades the sheer number of tourists to the city has strained its 200 or so hotels to capacity, and brought about a slide in standards among the more cynical hoteliers (who know they are guaranteed customers however grim their properties). Prices are also higher than in most of Italy (see panel opposite), and reservations are now a virtual necessity all year around (panel ► 66). Noise, location, and actually finding a room are other important considerations (see panels ► 67–69).

65

Mid-Range Hotels

RESERVATIONS

It is now almost essential to reserve a room in Venice for July and August, and wise to do so during the rest of the peak season, which officially runs from March 15 to November 15 and from December 21 to January 6, and now in effect includes the period of *Carnevale* in February. Many hotels do not recognize a low season, however, and lower category hotels where you might have been able to negotiate cheaper off-season rates often close during the winter. Some hotels accept credit-card reservations over the phone, but it is always best (having phoned or faxed first) to send a firm deposit in the mail. Follow this up with a confirmation of receipt and another call or fax a few days before departure to confirm your reservation.

AGLI ALBORETTI **

This 19-room hotel was added to the fine restaurant downstairs. Attractively located on a tree-lined street and convenient to the Accademia and Zattere. Rooms are modern and stylish, if a little small, and there is a pleasant garden. Extremely popular, especially with U.S. and U.K. visitors.

➕ E13 ✉ Rio Terrà Sant'Agnese-Antonio Foscarini, Dorsoduro 884 ☎ 041 523 0058; fax 041 521 0158 🚢 Accademia or Zattere 1, 52, 82

AMERICAN ***

A 29-room hotel two minutes' walk from the Accademia, on a small canal away from the crowds. Rooms vary in price and quality but most have a lot of wood and period touches. Lovely terrace and vine-shaded breakfast area.

➕ E13 ✉ Fondamenta Bragadin, Rio di San Vio, Dorsoduro 628 ☎ 041 520 4733; fax 041 520 4048 🚢 Accademia 1, 82

BOSTON ***

This 42-room hotel is on one of Venice's main shopping streets within easy reach of Piazza San Marco. Rooms vary in terms of furnishings and views; most are smallish, but comfortable and well-designed.

➕ G12 ✉ Calle dei Fabbri, San Marco 848 ☎ 041 528 7665; fax 041 522 6628 🚢 Rialto or Vallaresso 1, 82

CASANOVA ***

This comfortable hotel has 44 rooms and is in the heart of the shopping district close to Piazza San Marco. Mostly modern bedrooms but the public spaces have fine old furniture and vast antique mirrors.

➕ G12 ✉ Frezzeria, San Marco 1284 ☎ 041 520 6855; fax 041 520 6413 🚢 Vallaresso 1, 82

CLUB CRISTAL

A pleasant bed-and-breakfast of three-star standard in a quiet street near the Campo dei Gesuiti, with a pretty roof terrace for evening meals on request. English owners. Five spacious rooms, plus annexe accommodations.

➕ G10 ✉ Calle Zanardi, Cannaregio 4133 ☎ 041 523 7194 or 020 7722 5060 in the U.K.; fax 041 521 2705 🚢 Ca' d'Oro 1

DO POZZI ***

Quiet 29-room hotel in a pleasant courtyard square off Calle Larga (Viale) XXII Marzo. The style is a mixture of modern and antique; some rooms are a touch cramped.

➕ F13–G13 ✉ Corte dei Due Pozzi, San Marco 2373 ☎ 041 520 7855; fax 041 522 9413 🚢 Santa Maria del Giglio or Vallaresso 1, 82

FALIER **

A small, well-presented hotel in a part of town that is less busy, but still convenient to Santa Maria Gloriosa dei Frari and the Scuola Grande di San Rocco. Some of the 19 rooms (13 with private bathrooms) are small, but all are elegant and tidy, and prices are reasonable.

+ D11 **✉** Salizzada San Pantalon, Santa Croce 130 **☎** 041 710882; fax 041 520 6554 **🚤** Ferrovia or San Tomà 1, 52, 82

FLORA ***

This 44-room hotel has a well-deserved reputation, thanks to its pleasant garden. Some rooms are rather small. Just off Calle Larga (Viale) XXII Marzo west of Piazza San Marco.
+ F13 **✉** Calle Bergamaschi, San Marco 2283a **☎** 041 520 5844; fax 041 522 8217 **🚤** Santa Maria del Giglio 1

KETTE ***

Quiet location just southeast of La Fenice opera house. Some of the 70 rooms are small for the price, but rates can be reasonable off-season.
+ F12 **✉** Piscina San Moisè, San Marco 2053 **☎** 041 520 7766; fax 041 522 8964 **🚤** Vallaresso or Santa Maria del Giglio 1, 82

LA CALCINA ***

The waterfront location of this 29-room hotel—best known as the house where the Victorian artist and writer John Ruskin spent much of his Venetian sojourn—may not be to all tastes, but you are in an interesting area of the city well away from the bustle of central Venice.
+ E13–E14 **✉** Fondamenta Zattere ai Gesuati, Dorsoduro 780 **☎** 041 206466 or 041 520 6466; fax 041 522 7045 **🚤** Zattere 52, 82

LA FENICE ET DES ARTISTES ***

Pleasant hotel (once the home of painter Lorenzo Lotto) with 69 rooms divided into two buildings: rooms are modern and bland in one, elegant but faded in the other.
+ F12 **✉** Campiello Fenice, San Marco 1936 **☎** 041 523 2333; fax 041 520 3721 **🚤** Santa Maria del Giglio 1

PENSIONE SEGUSO **

This is a better choice than the nearby Calcina (see opposite), since almost all of its 36 traditionally furnished rooms have views across either the Giudecca or San Vio canals.
+ E13–E14 **✉** Fondamenta Zattere ai Gesuati, Dorsoduro 779 **☎** 041 528 6858; fax 041 522 2340 **🚤** Zàttere 52, 82

SAN CASSIANO-CA' FAVRETTO ***

A lovely hotel full of charm, in a converted 14th-century *palazzo* on the Grand Canal almost opposite the Ca' d'Oro. Half the 35 rooms face the Grand Canal; the rest look on to a side canal.
+ F10 **✉** Calle della Rosa, Santa Croce 2232 **☎** 041 524 1768; fax 041 721033 **🚤** San Stae 1

SANTA MARINA ***

Comfortable 20-room hotel opened in 1990 (the functional 8-room annexe is newer). It lies off the tourist trail, but is still extremely convenient to shopping and major sights. Bright rooms in Venetian period style.
+ H11 **✉** Campo di Santa Marina, Castello 6068 **☎** 041 523 9202; fax 041 520 0907 **🚤** Rialto 1, 82

NOISE

Although Venice is remarkably quiet, it still has its fair share of nocturnal traffic—even without cars. Church bells clang through the night and pedestrian chatter in the main alleys and streets is amplified in the close quarters. Traffic on the main canals can also be surprisingly noisy, and refuse boats, *vaporetti*, and food suppliers start up very early. This can put a different complexion on that apparently desirable room overlooking the Grand Canal.

Budget Hotels

LOCATION

Venice's best hotels line the Grand Canal near San Marco; the least expensive lie in the slightly grubby streets around the station and Lista di Spagna. Other concentrations of hotels are near the Rialto and in Dorsoduro, the latter being one of the city's less touristy locations. You will find the odd hotel in quiet backstreets, but there is no such thing as the "undiscovered gem." In a city as compact as Venice, however, even "poor" hotels are rarely far from the sights. Be certain when making reservations to find the hotel's exact location—the street name as well as number—and remember that you may well need to carry your luggage some distance.

AI DO MORI *

A friendly 11-room hotel with just eight bathrooms in a busy spot close to San Marco. Prices vary for different rooms: the best on the upper floors are small but have views over the Basilica di San Marco and the Torre dell' Orologio. Lower floor rooms are larger in a modern and simple style.

➕ G12–H12 ✉ Calle Larga San Marco, San Marco 658 ☎ 041 520 4817 or 041 528 9293; fax 041 520 5328 🚤 Vallaresso or San Zaccaria 1, 52, 82

ALEX *

This hotel's excellent location near Santa Maria Gloriosa dei Frari and the Scuola Grande di San Rocco makes up for the slightly tired and rather dated 11 rooms.

➕ E11 ✉ Rio Terrà Frari, San Polo 2606 ☎ 041 523 1341; fax 041 523 1341 🚤 San Tomà 1, 82

ANTICO CAPON *

Seven simple rooms (six with bathroom) above a good pizzeria-restaurant (➤ 74) on one of Venice's most informal squares. Excellent location for sightseeing in Frari and Scuola Grande di San Rocco area.

➕ D12 ✉ Campo Santa Margherita, Dorsoduro 3004/b ☎ 041 528 5292; fax 041 528 5292 🚤 San Tomà or Ca' Rezzonico 1, 82

CA' FOSCARI *

This relaxed and well-appointed hotel has ten rooms (none with private bathroom) and is hidden away in a little alley just south of San Tomà and Santa Maria Gloriosa dei Frari.

➕ E12 ✉ Calle della Frescada, Dorsoduro 3888 ☎ 041 710817 or 041 710401; fax 041 710817 🚤 San Tomà or Ca' Rezzonico 1, 82

CANADA **

This immaculate 25-room hotel has several singles. The best room (a double) has its own roof terrace, but you need to reserve it well in advance. In the heart of the city between the Rialto and Campo Santa Maria Formosa.

➕ G11 ✉ Campo San Lio, Castello 5659 ☎ 041 522 9912; fax 041 523 5852 🚤 Rialto 1, 82

DA BRUNO **

An excellent location close to the Rialto outweighs the small size of the hotel's 32 rooms.

➕ G11–H11 ✉ Salizzada San Lio, Castello 5726/a ☎ 041 523 0452; fax 041 522 1157 🚤 Rialto 1, 82

PANTALON ***

Just east of San Pantalon on a bustling little shopping street, this 15-room hotel has been renovated, pushing up its once bargain price to the top of the budget range. Near the Accademia, Santa Maria Gloriosa dei Frari, the Scuola Grande di San Rocco, and the attractive squares of Campo San Polo and Campo Santa Margherita.

➕ D12 ✉ Crosera San Pantalon, Dorsoduro 3942 ☎ 041 710 896; fax 041 718683 🚤 San Tomà 1, 82

DONI *

Intimate hotel in a convenient and attractive location between the Basilica and San Zaccaria, away from busy Piazza San Marco. The best of the 13 clean, simple rooms (none with private bathroom) overlook the Riva del Vin or the small garden.

🔲 H12 ✉ Fondamenta del Vin, off Salizzada San Provolo, Castello 4656 ☎ 041 522 4267; fax 041 522 4267 🚤 San Zaccaria 1, 52, 82

FIORITA *

Very pretty and popular hotel in a quaint square (used for breakfast in summer) just north of Santo Stefano. The ten rooms (eight with private bath) have wood beamed ceilings and plain furnishings.

🔲 F12 ✉ Campiello Nuovo, San Marco 3457/a ☎ 041 523 4754; fax 041 522 8043 🚤 Accademia or Sant'Angelo 1 82

MESSNER **

In a quiet corner of Dorsoduro, close to the church of Santa Maria della Salute. There is a lovely garden and 32 large modern rooms. Try to stay in the main hotel rather than the nearby annexe or *dipendenza*.

🔲 F13 ✉ Rio Terrà del Spezier, Dorsoduro 216 ☎ 041 522 7443; fax 041 522 7266 🚤 Santa Maria della Salute 1

MONTIN *

Much of this popular hotel's fame derives from the well-known and expensive restaurant of the same name downstairs.

The ten rooms (some with private bathroom) are pleasant, and larger and more comfortable than the one-star classification suggests.

🔲 D13 ✉ Fondamenta di Borgo, Dorsoduro 1147 ☎ 041 522 7151; fax 041 520 0255 🚤 Ca' Rezzonico or Accademia 1, 82

REMEDIO *

This 12-room hotel is on a tranquil side-street, in an excellent central location 100 yards from Piazza San Marco. The furniture is simple and the views unexceptional, but the hotel is clean and the staff welcoming.

🔲 H12 ✉ Calle del Rimedio, Castello 4412 ☎ 041 520 6232; fax 041 521 0485 🚤 Vallaresso 1, 82

SAN SAMUELE *

Some of the ten rooms at this welcoming hotel are basic, but the quality is much better than in many in this price range. Excellent location just north of Santo Stefano.

🔲 E12 ✉ Salizzada San Samuele, San Marco 3358 ☎ 041 522 8045; fax 041 522 8045 🚤 Sant'Angelo 1

SILVA *

Friendly 25-room hotel (with nine bathrooms) just north of Piazza San Marco between San Zaccaria and Santa Maria Formosa, on one of Venice's most attractive waterways.

🔲 H12 ✉ Fondamenta del Rimedio, Castello 4423 ☎ 041 522 7643/523 7892; fax 041 528 6817 🚤 San Zaccaria 1, 52, 82

FINDING A ROOM

By far the best thing to do is to plan ahead and reserve a room in advance (panel ► 66). If you arrive in Venice without accommodations do not accept rooms from touts at the station unless you are desperate: most work for generally less salubrious hotels nearby. If you are tempted, ignore their inevitably warm reassurances and find out exactly where the hotel is, how much the room will cost, whether it has a private bathroom, and whether the cost of breakfast is additional. Otherwise, join the lines for rooms at the tourist offices at the train station, Tronchetto, the Autorimessa car park in Piazzale Roma, at Marco Polo Airport, or at the Mestre-Marghera exit of the A4 expressway. Better, call the AVA (Venetian Hotelier's Association) who will book a room for you free of charge (☎ 041 785 016 or 041 715 288). In desperation, you could take a train to Padua (30 minutes). Unless you are unable to find a room in the right price bracket in Venice, do not stay in Mestre, the ugly and largely industrial town on the mainland.

Expensive Restaurants

Restaurants on the following pages are in three price categories:

Expensive	over 52 euros; L100,000
Mid-range	34–52 euros; L65–100,000
Budget	34 euros; under L65,000

HARRY'S BAR

This famous bar and restaurant was founded in 1931 when, according to legend, a now-forgotten American ("Harry") remarked to hotel barman Giuseppe Cipriani that Venice lacked for nothing except a good bar. The enterprising Cipriani duly sought financial backing, found an old rope store near Piazza San Marco, and Harry's Bar was born. It is now a place of high prices, good food, and great cocktails, and–in the words of writer Gore Vidal–"a babble of barbaric voices…the only place for Americans in acute distress to go for comfort and advice…"

AL COVO

Charming two-roomed restaurant in a calm, romantic, and tasteful setting. It is usually possible to eat out in the adjacent little square in summer. The service is generally warm and polite—the owner's wife at front of house is American—while the highly accomplished cooking focuses on traditional Venetian recipes using the best ingredients. Fish dishes predominate the regularly changing menu (when there is one), servings are small, the cooking fresh and refined, and the wine list is good. A fine alternative to the more bustling Corte Sconta nearby (▶ 72). With only 50 seats, be sure to reserve ahead.
🔲 J12 ✉ Campiello della Pescaria, Castello 3968 ☎ 041 522 3812 ⓖ Closed Wed, Thu, and two weeks in Aug and Jan ⛴ Arsenale 1

ANTICA MONTIN

This venerable restaurant has been famous for several decades and is popular with the rich and famous, although today it depends somewhat on its former reputation. The quality of food is now once again touching former heights; an evocative place to eat, either in the painting-lined dining room or on the shaded outside terrace to the rear.
🔲 D13 ✉ Fondamenta di Borgo, Dorsoduro 1147 ☎ 041 522 7151 ⓖ Closed Tue evening, Wed ⛴ Zattere or Ca' Rezzonico 1, 52, 82

ANTICO MARTINI

Established in the 18th century, The Martini has long been one of the city's most stylish restaurants. Classic Venetian cuisine with seafood playing a key role. The terrace overlooks La Fenice, and the wine list numbers 300 labels. Meals are served until 1AM, unusually late in Venice.
🔲 F12 ✉ Campo San Fantin, San Marco 1983 ☎ 041 522 4121 ⓖ Closed Tue, Wed lunch; dinner only Dec–mid-Mar ⛴ Santa Maria del Giglio 1

DA FIORE

This small, highly acclaimed restaurant produces excellent Venetian cuisine, cooked up by self-taught owners. Since appearing as one of the "world's best" restaurants in the American publication *International Herald Tribune*, it has become extremely difficult to get a table. Hard to find.
🔲 E11 ✉ Calle del Scaleter, San Polo 2002/a ☎ 041 721308 ⓖ Closed Sun, Mon ⛴ San Stae or San Silvestro 1

DANIELI TERRACE

Venice's upscale hotels all have fine restaurants and the Danieli is no exception. Refined Venetian and international cooking is served with panache on the stylish terrace overlooking the Grand Canal. Fine service and an excellent wine list, all at high prices.
🔲 H12 ✉ Riva degli Schiavoni-Calle delle Rasse, Castello 4196 ☎ 041 522 6480 ⛴ San Zaccaria 1, 4, 52, 82

DO FORNI

A slightly self-conscious restaurant known as one of *the* places to eat among locals and tourists alike. One dining room is furnished rustically and the other fashioned like an opulent *Orient Express* cabin. The number of tables and the menu have grown with the restaurant's success, but despite the chaos the food remains good—although at inflated prices.

➕ G12 ✉ Calle dei Specchieri, San Marco 457 ☎ 041 523 0663 🚤 Vallaresso 1, 82

HARRY'S BAR

This legendary establishment is best known for its celebrity status. The restaurant upstairs serves reliable fare (although it can be very good, many say it is not what it used to be), while snacks can be ordered at the downstairs bar. This is the place to come for cocktails—the Bellini was invented here.

➕ G13 ✉ Calle Vallaresso, San Marco 1323 ☎ 041 528 5777 🚤 Vallaresso 1, 82

HARRY'S DOLCI

What began as a glorified cake- and coffee-shop offshoot of Harry's Bar (see above) has turned into a restaurant every bit as good (and almost as expensive) as its parent. The refined food is Venetian, while the atmosphere is chic without being at all intimidating.

➕ D14 ✉ Fondamenta San Biagio, Giudecca 773 ☎ 041 522 4844 ⏱ Apr–Oct: daily 10:30–3PM, 7:30–10:30PM. Nov–Mar: closed Tue 🚤 Sant'Eufemia 52, 82

LA CARAVELLA

The interior of this restaurant, one of two in the Saturnia hotel (➤ 65), is decked out in the manner of a Venetian galley. The over-the-top decor fails to detract from the normally outstanding food, but it can be prone to lapses. The cooking has international as well as Venetian touches.

➕ F13 ✉ Calle Larga (Viale) XXII Marzo, San Marco 2398 ☎ 041 520 8901 ⏱ Closed Wed in winter 🚤 Santa Maria del Giglio 1

LOCANDA CIPRIANI

The fine food served in this wonderful setting—facing the island's two churches—makes up for the hefty prices and pretentious look.

➕ Off map ✉ Fondamenta dei Borgononi-Piazza Santa Fosca 29, Torcello ☎ 041 730150 ⏱ Closed Tue in winter and Jan 🚤 Torcello 12, 14

POSTE VECIE

Ingredients could hardly be fresher than at this appealing fish restaurant in an old post house alongside the Rialto's Pescheria fish market. The cooking is refined, but can be variable, and there's a good wine list. Reputedly founded in 1500.

➕ F10–F11 ✉ Campo della Pescaria, San Polo 1608 ☎ 041 721822 ⏱ Closed Tue and four weeks in Jul and Aug 🚤 Rialto 1, 3, 82

WINES

Most of Venice's wine comes from the Veneto region on the mainland. Its best-known wines are the usually unexceptional Soave (white), and Valpolicella and Bardolino (reds). More interesting whites include Soave Classico, Bianco di Custoza, Tocai, Pinot Grigio, and the wines of the Breggaze region. The best white of all is Prosecco, a delicious dry sparkling wine often drunk as an aperitif. Interesting reds include Raboso, the wines of the Colle Berici and Lison-Pramaggiore regions, and two excellent dessert wines: Amarone and Recioto della Valpolicella.

Mid-Range Restaurants

FIRST COURSES

Venice's best-known first courses are *sarde in saôr* (sardines in a cold onion and vinegar marinade) or a simple mixed plate of seafood (*antipasto di mare*). *Prosciutto San Daniele* is the region's best ham. Pasta is available, usually with seafood–try *spaghetti alle vongole* (pasta with clams)–but most locals prefer rice, notably *risi e bisi* (rice, peas and ham) or risotto with seafood (*risotto di mare* or *dei pescatori*), mushrooms (*funghi*), vegetables, chicken, and ham (*alla sbirraglia*), or flavored with cuttlefish ink (*risotto in nero*). Tripe, snails, and quail may also feature. Fish soup (*brodetto* or *zuppa di mare*) is another popular first course, as is pasta and bean soup (*pasta e fasioli*).

AGLI ALBORETTI

Convenient to the Accademia, just two minutes' walk away, this restaurant takes its name from the trees (*alberi*) outside. It is pretty inside and out, and in summer you can eat in a pergola-shaded courtyard.

✚ E13 ✉ Rio Terrà Antonio Foscarini-Sant'Agnese, Dorsoduro 882 ☎ 041 523 0058 🕐 Closed Thu lunch and Wed 🚤 Accademia 1, 3, 4, 82

AL MASCARON

A nice old bar-trattoria with a brisk, informal atmosphere, a beamed ceiling, and a line of old black and white photos on the walls. Venetian fish and seafood cooking is served at the brown, heavy wood tables on paper table cloths. So popular—reservations are essential—that the owners have opened the similar Alla Mascareta for wine and snacks a few doors down at 5183.

✚ H11 ✉ Calle Lunga Santa Maria Formosa, Castello 5525 ☎ 041 522 5995 or 041 523 0744 🕐 Closed Sun; Alla Mascareta open evenings only 🚤 Rialto 1, 3, 4, 82

AI MERCANTI

Ai Mercanti is situated close to the Rialto's fish market, a perfect location for a restaurant that is devoted mainly to fish and seafood. Tasteful and elegant, it makes a good alternative if the better-known Alla Madonna (see below) is full. Dishes include *risotto alle vongole* and *spaghetti con melanzane e calamaretti*.

✚ G12 ✉ Calle dei Fuséri, San Marco 4346/a ☎ 041 523 8269 🕐 Closed Sun, Mon lunch and Aug 1–15 🚤 Rialto 1, 3, 82

AL CONTE PESCAOR

A wonderful tiny fish restaurant that caters to Venetians despite its proximity to Piazza San Marco.

✚ G12 ✉ Piscina San Zulian, San Marco 544 ☎ 041 522 1483 🕐 Closed Sun and Jan during winter 🚤 Vallaresso 1, 3, 4, 82

ALLA MADONNA

One of Venice's most authentic restaurants, and one of the oldest in the city—it has the look of a Venetian restaurant of 30 years ago. A popular favorite for business meetings and family celebrations. The good food is rigorously Venetian, including such typical dishes as *sarde in saôr*, *zuppa di pesce*, and *ai frutte di mare*. The dining area is roomy and the service, if sometimes brusque, efficiently run.

✚ F11 ✉ Calle della Madonna, San Polo 594 ☎ 041 522 3824 🕐 Closed Wed and two weeks in Aug 🚤 Rialto 1, 3, 82

CORTE SCONTA

Many Venetians and visitors alike rate the Corte Sconta as their favorite among the city's restaurants, despite its slightly peripheral location (close to the Arsenale). It is fairly small (just 70 seats) and is always busy, but nonetheless is very pleasant, while the cooking and seafood are rarely less than excellent. No menu as such, so try to follow waiting staff's recommendations. A small garden is open for outdoor eating in summer. Somewhat hard to find.

➕ J12 ✉ Calle del Pestrin, Castello 3886 ☎ 041 522 7024 ⏰ Closed Sun and Mon 🚤 Arsenale 1

DA IGNAZIO

This fairly small and predominantly fish restaurant lies just east of Campo San Tomà, and has the atmosphere of a restaurant from the 1950s. Garden for alfresco dining in summer.

➕ E11 ✉ Calle Saoneri, San Polo 2749 ☎ 041 523 4852 ⏰ Closed Sat and three weeks in Jul and Aug 🚤 San Tomà 1, 82

DA REMIGIO

Neighborhood trattorias are a dying breed in Venice, so this authentic little restaurant, despite a redecoration that has removed some old-fashioned touches, is a find. It has just 40 seats, so reserve or arrive early to share a table. The food is reliable and homey, and the wine list is short but adequate.

➕ J12 ✉ Salizzada dei Greci, Castello 3416 ☎ 041 523 0089 ⏰ Closed Mon evening and Tue 🚤 San Zaccaria or Arsenale 1, 4, 52, 82

FIASCHETTERIA TOSCANA

Despite the "Toscana" in its name, the menu at this favorite restaurant established in 1956 includes classic Venetian dishes and seafood. Excellent

selection of wines.

➕ G11 ✉ Salizzada San Giovanni Cristostomo, Cannaregio 5719 ☎ 041 528 5281 ⏰ Closed Tue and three weeks in Jul 🚤 Rialto 1, 3, 82

FIORE

This thoroughly local trattoria has lots of color, with a popular bar serving snacks as well as an intimate restaurant. Do not confuse it with Da Fiore in San Polo (➤ 70). Just off Campo Santo Stefano (Campo Francesco Morosini).

➕ F12 ✉ Calle delle Botteghe, San Marco 3460 ☎ 041 523 5310 ⏰ Closed Tue 🚤 San Samuele 1

VINI DA ARTURO

Virtually the only fine restaurant in Venice that concentrates on meat dishes rather than fish. Good wine list and a tiny pleasant wood-paneled dining room.

➕ F12 ✉ Rio Terrà degli Assassini, San Marco 3656 ☎ 041 528 6974 ⏰ Closed Sun 🚤 Sant'Angelo 1

VINI DA GIGIO

A pretty, relaxed, and romantic restaurant on a peaceful canal: just two simple rooms with beams and old wooden cabinets. Venetian cooking including fish and meat dishes, and a short, well-chosen wine list. Good for lunch or dinner.

➕ F10 ✉ Fondamenta della Chiesa-San Felice, Cannaregio 3628a ☎ 041 528 5140 ⏰ Closed Sun evening, Mon, Jan, and three weeks in Aug 🚤 Ca' d'Oro 1

ENTRÉES

Venice's most famous entrée is calf's liver and onions (*fegato alla veneziana*), although fish and seafood form the city's main culinary staples. Mussels (*cozze* or *peoci*) from the lagoon are common, together with cuttlefish (*seppie*) and fish such as sole (*sogliola*), red mullet (*triglia*), mullet (*céfalo*), sea bream (*orata*), monkfish (*coda di rospo*), and mackerel (*sgombro*). Fish is best eaten grilled (*alla griglia* or *ai ferri*). For a variety of fish and seafood opt for a *fritto di pesce* or *fritto misto di mare*, a plate of mixed fried fish and seafood. To round off a meal, sample Venice's well-known *tiramisù* (literally "pick me up"), usually a rum liqueur-laced pudding of sponge, mascarpone cheese, eggs, and chocolate.

Budget Restaurants

PAYING

The check (*il conto*) usually includes a cover charge per person (*pane e coperto*) and a 10–15 percent service charge (*servizio*). Restaurants are required by law to give you a proper receipt (*una ricevuta*). Always look at your check carefully, especially if—as still happens—it is an illegible scrawl on a piece of paper (strictly speaking illegal). Skipping *antipasti* and desserts will reduce costs—go to a *gelateria* for an ice cream instead. Fixed-price tourist menus (*menù turistico*) usually include a basic pasta, main course, fruit, and half-bottles of wine and water. Food quality is often indifferent—you will probably find many of the same dishes listed on the menu in a budget trattoria as in most expensive restaurants. The difference is primarily one of ambience and detail. The *prezzo fisso* menu usually excludes cover, service, and beverages. Check what is included in the price.

Remember that inexpensive snacks and meals are also available in cafés and wine bars (➤ 76–78).

ACIUGHETA

The "Little Anchovy" pizzeria-trattoria is one of the best places in the budget price-range near Piazza San Marco.

🚇 H12 ⊠ Campo Santi Filippo e Giacomo, Castello 4357 ☎ 041 522 4292 🕒 Closed Wed in winter 🚏 San Zaccaria 1, 52, 82

AI PROMESSI SPOSI

This friendly bar-restaurant serves up mainly fish dishes that are both inexpensive and come in huge portions. The bar snacks are also excellent and even less inexpensive.

🚇 G10 ⊠ Calle dell'Oca, Cannaregio 4367 ☎ 041 522 8609 🕒 Closed Wed 🚏 Ca' d'Oro 1

AL GATTO NERO

This traditional trattoria is the best place on Burano for simple, reasonably priced food. Outside tables by the canal overlook the old fish market.

🚇 L2 ⊠ Calle Stivallo-Fondamenta Giudecca, Burano 88 ☎ 041 730120 🕒 Closed Mon 🚏 Burano 12, 14

ALLA RIVETTA

An inexpensive but good trattoria close to Piazza San Marco that makes a pleasant alternative to the nearby Aciugheta (see above). Small and often very busy.

🚇 H12 ⊠ Ponte San Provolo, near Campo SS Filippo e Giacomo, Castello 4625 ☎ 041 528 7302 🕒 Closed Mon 🚏 San Zaccaria 1, 52, 82

ALLA ZUCCA

Venetians come to this informal trattoria, tucked away near San Giacomo dell'Orio, when they want a change from Venetian cooking. Dishes are inventive, and often have an Oriental twist. Pleasant service from the mostly female staff. Good vegetarian options.

🚇 E10 ⊠ Ponte del Megio, Santa Croce 1762 ☎ 041 524 1570 🕒 Closed Sun 🚏 San Stae 1

ALLE OCHE

Just south of the quiet little square of Campo San Giacomo dell'Orio. Very popular, so reserve or arrive early to secure a table outside, and enjoy one of the many pizzas.

🚇 E10–E11 ⊠ Calle del Tintor, San Polo 1552 ☎ 041 524 1161 🕒 Closed Mon 🚏 Riva di Biasio 1

ANTICO CAPON

A pleasant location on one of Venice's most attractive squares, plus pizzas cooked in a wood-fired oven (a rarity in fire-conscious Venice). In summer rows of tables are laid out on the piazza.

🚇 D12 ⊠ Campo Santa Margherita, Dorsoduro 3004/b ☎ 041 528 5292 🕒 Closed Wed 🚏 San Tomà or Ca' Rezzonico 1, 82

DONA ONESTA

The "Honest Woman" lives up to its name with fine food at budget prices. It is now becoming

increasingly well known,
however, so try to reserve
a table in its single small
dining room. Overlooks a
little canal midway
between San Pantalon and
San Tomà.

➕ E12 ✉ Calle della Donna
Onesta, Dorsoduro ☎ 041 522
9586 🕐 Closed Sun 🚏 San
Tomà 1, 82

OSTERIA AI CACCIATORI

A pleasant old-fashioned
establishment on Murano's
main canal in a street
known for its glass shops.
One of the few places to
eat on the island.

➕ K7–L6 ✉ Fondamenta dei
Vetrai, Murano 69 🚏 Faro or
Colonna 12, 42

ROSTICCERIA SAN BARTOLOMEO

A large self-service place
that is good for snacks,
especially at lunchtime.
There is no cover charge
or service downstairs (the
restaurant upstairs has
almost the same food but
at a higher price). Near
the Rialto, off Campo San
Bartolomeo.

➕ G11 ✉ Calle della Bissa,
San Marco 5424 ☎ 041 522
3569 🕐 Closed Mon 🚏 Rialto
1, 3, 82

TAVERNA SAN TROVASO

Not the best cuisine in
the city, yet it has reliable
cooking at reasonable
prices. Popular with
Venetians, and its position
west of the Accademia
attracts plenty of passing
trade. Make a reservation
to be sure of a place
(especially for Sunday
lunch).

➕ E13 ✉ Fondamenta Priuli,
Dorsoduro 1016 ☎ 041 520
3703 🕐 Closed Mon
🚏 Accademia 1, 3, 4, 82

TRATTORIA SAN TOMÀ

Both the pizzas and
trattoria food served here
are good, but this
restaurant's best attraction
is its location on Campo
San Tomà, just one
minute south of
Santa Maria Gloriosa dei
Frari and the Scuola
Grande di San Rocco.

➕ E12 ✉ Campo San Tomà,
San Polo 2864 ☎ 041 710586
🕐 Closed Tue in winter 🚏 San
Tomà 1, 82

VECIO FRITOLIN

A trattoria with old
wooden chairs, wonderful
glass lamps, ancient
mirrors, an age-darkened
interior, and brown,
worn checkered plastic
tablecloths. Locals crowd
in for fine snacks and a
handful of main and pasta
dishes (largely fish-based)
that change daily.

➕ F10–F11 ✉ Calle della
Regina, Santa Croce 2262 ☎ 041
522 2881 🕐 Closed Sun, Mon
lunch, and Aug 🚏 San Stae 1

VIVALDI

This small, relaxed, and
pleasantly Venetian place
produces simple hot dishes
that can either be eaten
informally at the front or
sitting down at a few tables
to the rear, where more
ambitious (and more
expensive) meals are also
available.

➕ F11 ✉ Calle della
Madonnetta, San Polo 1457
☎ 041 523 8185 🕐 Closed
Sun 🚏 San Silvestro 1

DRINKS

Venice's water is perfectly safe
to drink, though Venetians
prefer mineral water (*acqua
minerale*)—either sparkling
(*gassata*) or still (*liscia,
naturale*, or *non gassata*).
Bottles come in one liter (*un
litro* or *una bottiglia*) or half-
liter (*mezzo litro* or *mezza
bottiglia*) sizes. Bottled fruit
juice is *un succo di frutta*,
available in pear (*pera*),
apricot (*albiccoca*), peach
(*pesca*), and other flavors.
Fresh juice is *una spremuta*,
while milk shake is *un frullato*,
or *un frappé* if made with ice
cream. *Lemon soda* is a
popular and refreshing bitter-
lemon drink. Ice is *ghiaccio*,
and a slice of lemon is *uno
spicchio di limone*.

Cafés, Bars & Gelaterie

ETIQUETTE

The procedure when standing up in a bar is to pay for what you want at the cash desk (*la cassa*) and take your receipt (*lo scontrino*) to the bar, where you repeat your order (a tip slapped down on the bar works wonders with the service). Do *not* then take your drink and sit at outside tables, as you almost always pay a premium to sit down when you order through a waiter. Sitting, a single purchase allows you to watch the world go by almost indefinitely. Ice cream (*un gelato*) comes in a cone (*un cono*) or a tub (*una coppa*): specify which you want, along with a price (quantity and tub size rise in price intervals from about 1–2 euros; L2,000–4,000). You are also often asked if you want cream (*panna*) on top, which is usually free.

AI VINI PADOVANI

A good, simple, and authentic Venetian bar with enthusiastic young owners: there is a stand-up counter with a larger room to the right for light meals and snacks.

➕ E12 ✉ Calle dei Cerchieri, Dorsoduro 1280 🚢 Ca' Rezzonico 1

CA' D'ORO

This wonderfully fusty and very Venetian place has been owned by the same family for over a century. Also known as La Vedova ("The Widow"), it serves snacks and basic hot meals.

➕ G10 ✉ Calle del Pistor-Ramo Ca' d'Oro, Cannaregio 3912-3952 ⏰ Closed Sun and Thu 🚢 Ca' d'Oro 1

CAFFÈ DEI FRARI

If you do not want to walk to Ciak (see below), try this lively bar just across the bridge in front of Santa Maria Gloriosa dei Frari. A favorite with university students.

➕ E11 ✉ Fondamenta dei Frari, San Polo 2564 🚢 San Tomà 1, 82

CAUSIN

Opened in 1928, this is one of several excellent cafés on Venice's nicest square. Great ice cream and plenty of outdoor tables.

➕ D12 ✉ Campo Santa Margherita, Dorsoduro 2996 ⏰ Closed Sat 🚢 Ca' Rezzonico 1

CIAK

Pleasant and relaxed bar after visiting Santa Maria Gloriosa dei Frari and the Scuola Grande di San Rocco. Used by everyone from gondoliers to society ladies. Good lunchtime snacks and sandwiches.

➕ E12 ✉ Campo San Tomà, San Polo 280 🚢 San Tomà 1, 82

FLORIAN

The oldest, prettiest, and most expensive of Venice's famous cafés has been serving customers since 1720. Prices are high, but treat yourself at least once for the experience and the chance to admire the lovely frescoed and mirrored interior.

➕ G12 ✉ Piazza San Marco, San Marco 56–59 ⏰ Closed Wed 🚢 Vallaresso 1, 82

GUANOTTO

A café and ice-cream parlor near the Teatro Goldoni that is also allegedly Venice's oldest *pasticceria*, or pastry shop, and is supposed to have invented the spritzer, a mix of white wine, bitters, and soda water. Also great for coffee and cocktails.

➕ G12 ✉ Ponte dell' Ovo, San Marco 4819 ⏰ Closed Sun in summer 🚢 Rialto 1, 82

HARRY'S DOLCI

This offshoot of Harry's Bar (➤ 71) began as a fancy coffee shop, but now serves meals as well. It remains a good place to treat yourself to a morning coffee or afternoon tea in refined but unintimidating surroundings.

➕ D14 ✉ Fondamenta San Biagio, Giudecca 773 ☎ 041 522 4844 ⏰ Apr–Oct: daily 10:30AM–3PM, 7:30–10:30PM. Nov–Mar: closed Tue 🚢 Sant'Eufemia 52, 82

IL CAFFÈ

Another appealing and photogenic little bar on Campo Santa Margherita. Its outside tables are a favorite place to soak up the sun and streetlife.

✠ D12 ✉ Campo Santa Margherita, Dorsoduro 2963 🕓 Closed Sun 🚤 Ca' Rezzonico 1

MARCHINI

This café-*pasticceria* just east of Campo Santo Stefano (Campo Francesco Morosini) is widely regarded as Venice's best. The window displays alone are worth a special visit.

✠ F12–F13 ✉ Ponte San Maurizio, San Marco 2769 🚤 Santa Maria del Giglio 1

NICO

Organize a walk or stroll in the San Polo or Dorsoduro districts so that you pass this small waterfront bar renowned for its ice cream, in particular a praline concoction known as *gianduiotto*.

✠ E14 ✉ Zattere ai Gesuati, Dorsoduro 922 🕓 Closed Thu 🚤 Zattere 52, 82

PAOLIN

The best café in one of Venice's nicest squares. Lots of outside tables, and some of the city's best ice cream.

✠ F12 ✉ Campo Santo Stefano (Campo Francesco Morosini), San Marco 2962 🕓 Closed Fri 🚤 Accademia 1, 82

PARADISO PERDUTO

A good choice of bar both day and night if you want to rub shoulders with the more arty and Bohemian of Venice's inhabitants. Lively late at night, and you'll find meals and snacks at shared wooden tables, and the occasional live music.

✠ F9 ✉ Fondamenta della Misericordia, Cannaregio 2540 🕓 Closed Wed 🚤 San Marcuola 1, 82

QUADRI

Not quite so famous or socially exalted as Florian (see opposite), Quadri was abandoned by Venetian high society in the 19th century because it was frequented by officers of the occupying Austrian army. However prices reach Florian's stratospheric levels.

✠ G12 ✉ Piazza San Marco, San Marco 120–4 🕓 Closed Mon 🚤 Vallaresso 1, 82

ROSA SALVA

Venice's best café chain has outlets city wide. Coffees and cakes are good, but the atmosphere a bit sterile and bland.

✠ G12 ✉ Campo San Luca, San Marco 🚤 Rialto 1, 3, 82;
✠ G11–G12 ✉ Merceria San Salvador, San Marco 951 🚤 Rialto 1, 3, 82;
✠ G12 ✉ Calle Fiubera, San Marco 🚤 Vallaresso 1, 82

VINO VINO

Rather more showy and smarter than some of Venice's humbler bars, this two-roomed spot close to La Fenice opera house has over 100 different wines to accompany its middling snacks and meals.

✠ F12 ✉ Ponte delle Veste, Calle delle Veste, San Marco 2007a 🕓 Closed Tue 🚤 Santa Maria del Giglio 1

COFFEE

At breakfast you will be served a milky *cappuccino*, said to be named after the brown robes and white cowls of Capuchin monks. During the rest of the day the locals' coffee of choice is the short, black *espresso* or *un caffè*. A longer *espresso* is a *lungo* or a *doppia* (double). American-style coffee (not as strong as the Italian brews) is *un caffè Americano*. Other varieties include iced coffee (*caffè freddo*), *caffè corretto* (with a dash of grappa or brandy), *caffè latte* (a milky coffee), and *caffè macchiato* (an *espresso* "stained" with a drop of milk). Note that Italians rarely drink *cappuccino* after midday—and never after a meal, when they opt for *espresso* or camomile tea (*una camomila*) instead.

Wine Bars

WINE BARS

Old-fashioned wine bars, or *bacari*, are a Venetian way of life. One of the city's more civilized habits is the custom of breaking up the day with an *ombra* ("shadow"), a small glass of wine that takes its name from the idea of escaping the heat of the sun for a restorative tipple. A small snack, or *cichetto*, usually accompanies the drink. An *enoteca* is a more refined bar, with a greater choice of wines and a range of reasonably priced snacks and hot meals.

AL VOLTO

Genuine wood-beamed *enoteca* north of Campo Manin. Good snacks and a staggering 1,300 different wines from Italy and the rest of the world.

F12 ⊠ Calle Cavalli, San Marco 4081 Closed Sun Rialto 1, 82

ANTICO DOLO

The Rialto market district has one of the city's largest selections of old-fashioned wine bars, this is one of the best. Excellent snacks (the tripe is famous) and a small but fine menu for evening meals.

F11 ⊠ Ruga Vecchia San Giovanni, San Polo 778 Closed Sun Rialto 1, 82

BOLDRIN

Excellent and spacious *enoteca* in the northern part of the city. Wine by the glass and hot snacks. Wonderfully mixed clientele—old ladies with little dogs to paint-spattered builders.

G11 ⊠ Salizzada San Chianciano, Cannaregio 5550 Closed Sun Rialto 1, 82

CANTINA DEL VINO GIÀ SCHIAVI

An old-fashioned wine bar that really looks the part, set almost opposite San Trovaso and one of Venice's few remaining gondola workshops.

E13 ⊠ Fondamenta Nani-Meravegie, Dorsoduro 992 Closed Sun Accademia, Zattere 1, 82

DO MORI

The most authentic and atmospheric of Venice's old-time *bacari*, in business since 1462. Always filled with locals, shoppers, and traders from the nearby Rialto markets. Good snacks; 350 wines. No seats or tables.

F11 ⊠ Calle do Mori, off Ruga Vecchia San Giovanni, San Polo 429 Closed Sun, Wed afternoon Rialto 1, 3, 82

DO SPADE

Not quite as hectic and nicely down-at-heel as the nearby Do Mori (see above), but almost as busy and equally authentic. Unlike its neighbor, it also has tables. Difficult to find.

F11 ⊠ Sottoportego Spade, off Calle Angelo, San Polo 860 Jul–Aug: Mon–Wed, Fri–Sat 9–2, 5–8; Thu 9–2. Sep–Jun: Mon–Wed, Fri–Sat 9–2, 5–11; Thu 9–2. Closed Sun Rialto 1, 82

OSTERIA AGLI ASSASSINI

This wine bar is off the beaten track between Campo Manin and Campo Sant'Angelo, and has a good selection of wines, light snacks, and basic meals.

F12 ⊠ Rio Terrà degli Assassini, San Marco 3695 Closed Sat lunch and Sun Sant'Angelo 1

OSTERIA ALLE BOTTEGHE

Lively and very busy wine bar, just north of Campo Santo Stefano (Campo Francesco Morosini). Plenty of wines and a small selection of snacks.

F12 ⊠ Calle delle Botteghe, San Marco Closed Sun Sant'Angelo or San Samuele 1, 82

Glass & Beads

ANTICLEA ANTIQUARIATO
This beautiful little store is a wonderful collection of antique Venetian beads and jewelry. The owner has spent a lifetime amassing her stock, the best of which is kept in countless small drawers around the walls. Beads of your choice can be made up on the spot into earrings or necklaces.
✚ H12 ✉ Campo San Provolo, Castello 4719a ☎ 041 528 6946 🚤 San Zaccaria 1, 52, 82

BAROVIER E TOSO
One of the better of the many glass showrooms on Murano, this family firm dates back to the 14th century and makes glass to traditional designs, drawing its inspiration from a private 26,000-piece collection of antique glass.
✚ K7–L6 ✉ Fondamenta dei Vetrai, Murano 28 ☎ 041 739049 🚤 Colonna or Faro 12, 42

L'ISOLA
Grotesque modern glass litters countless Venetian stores and souvenir stands. This store has some of the city's better contemporary designs, although you may still find some of them too far-fetched. As with much Venetian glass, prices can be surprisingly high.
✚ G12 ✉ Salizzada San Moisè, San Marco 1468 ☎ 041 523 1973 🚤 Vallaresso 1, 82

PAULY
Pauly has been selling the finest Venetian glass since 1866. Its warren of showrooms contain all manner of treasures, including antique pieces that can be copied to order. A little over half a million dollars will buy you the company's finest chandelier.
✚ K12 ✉ Ponte Consorzi, Calle Largo, Castello 4391 ☎ 041 520 9899 🚤 San Zaccaria 1, 52, 82

SALVIATI
Founded in 1866, Salviati is known for having provided the eye-catching mosaics on the facade of the Grand Canal's Palazzo Salviati, on the south bank close to the Palazzo Dario. There are outlets in Murano and in Venice proper in Piazza San Marco.
✚ F13 ✉ Fondamenta Radi 16 ☎ 041 522 4033 🚤 Colonna, Faro or Museo 12, 42

SEGUSO
Another of Murano's better and more established institutions, Seguso has been in business for several decades. Renowned for its copies of antique glass.
✚ L6 ✉ Fondamenta dei Vetrai, Murano 143 ☎ 041 739423 🚤 Colonna or Faro 12, 42

VENINI
A Murano institution since the 1930s attracting some of the top names in glass design. The designs are more upscale and daring than those of many producers.
✚ G12 ✉ Piazzetta dei Leoni (Piazzetta dei Leoncini), San Marco 314 ☎ 041 277 0389 🚤 Vallaresso 1, 82; ✚ K7–L6 ✉ Fondamenta dei Vetrai, Murano 47 ☎ 041 527 4870 or 041 739955 🚤 Colonna, Faro or Museo 12, 42

POISON DAGGERS
Murano glass was said to be so fine that it would shatter on coming into contact with even the smallest drop of poison. It was also used in the Venetian dagger, one of the Middle Ages' nastier weapons. Much loved by Venice's secret police, the dagger consisted of a razor-sharp blade of glass, sheathed in metal, which when sunk into a victim's body would snap off at the haft. The unfortunate's skin would close over the glass, leaving a wound apparently no more than an innocent graze at the point of entry.

Window-Shopping

WHERE TO LOOK

Fine stores can be found across Venice, but the city's better stores (especially for shoes and fashion) cluster in well-defined areas such as the Calle dei Fabbri (✚ G12); Calle dell'Ascensione-Calle Larga (Viale) XXII Marzo (✚ F13–G12); the Frezzeria (✚ G12); and the so-called Mercerie—San Zulian, d'Orologio and San Salvador—which run from Piazza San Marco to the Rialto (✚ G12)

DEPARTMENT STORES

The only large department store worthy of the name is the excellent COIN, which sells a wide range of fashion, toiletries, accessories, china, linen, gifts, and general goods. It occupies a large corner block on the east side of Salizzada San Giovanni Crisostomo between the Rialto and the church of San Giovanni Crisostomo (✚ G11).

EMILIO CECCATO

If there is one souvenir, over and above glass, that greets you at every turn in Venice, it is the fake and mass produced gondolier's straw hat. This unique little store sells the genuine article, together with gondoliers' garb— hats, tunics and trousers— to both gondoliers and curious foreigners.
✚ G11 ✉ Sottoportego di Rialto, San Polo 1617 ☎ 041 522 2700 🚤 Rialto 1, 82

EMPORIO ARMANI

No leading Italian city would be complete without a flagship store dedicated to one of the most famous names in Italian fashion. In Venice Armani is in one of the city's main shopping streets, a short walk from Piazza San Marco. The clothes are peerless, classic, and exquisitely cut.
✚ G12 ✉ Calle dei Fabbri, San Marco 989 ☎ 041 523 7808 🚤 Rialto 1, 82

FIORELLA

Hilarious and wonderfully original, Fiorella has Venice's best-dressed window: the store dummies, crafted in wood, represent life-sized models of former doges, each incongruously decked out in high heels and other slightly offbeat high fashion items.
✚ F12 ✉ Campo Santo Stefano (Campo Francesco Morosini), San Marco 2806 ☎ 041 520 9228 🚤 Accademia 1, 82

JESURUM

Factory-made (and often foreign-manufactured) lace has undercut and largely supplanted the famous traditional hand-made specialty from Burano (► 21). As a result, original and old-style lace is now extremely rare and expensive. These two stores, near the Rialto bridge and Piazza San Marco, have an excellent selection of both types, plus a fine collection of superb linens and lingerie. Other little stores selling lace, often at high prices, are dotted around the city. Place-settings and similar small pieces make excellent gifts.
✚ G11 ✉ Merceria del Capitello, San Marco 4857 ☎ 041 520 6177 🚤 Rialto 1, 82

LABORATORIO ARTIGIANO MASCHERE

This wonderful mask workshop, just east of Santi Giovanni e Paolo, is home to Giorgio Clanetti, scion of a family of puppet-makers, who was one of the first to resurrect the Venetian mask-making tradition. Other papier-mâché objects like boxes and frames are also sold.
✚ H11–J11 ✉ Barbaria delle Tole, Castello 6657 ☎ 041 522 3110 🚤 Ospedale 23, 52

LAURA BIAGIOTTA

One of the big names in Italian fashion, in the heart of one of the city's most exclusive shopping streets, which runs west from Piazza San Marco.
✚ F13–G12 ✉ Calle Larga (Viale) XXII Marzo, San Marco 2400/a ☎ 041 520 3401 🚤 Vallaresso 1, 82

MARFORIO

Founded in 1875 and run by the same family for five generations, this store claims to be Italy's oldest and largest retailer of leather goods. The quality and range are both excellent, with bags and other leather goods from all the top names in the fashion firmament.

➕ G11 ✉ Campo San Salvador, San Marco 5033 ☎ 522 5734 🚤 Rialto 1, 82

MISSIAGLIA

Missiaglia is widely considered the city's finest jeweler. White-and-yellow gold settings with colored stones are the main specialty: styles are mostly classic, but with occasional more contemporary pieces. With a Piazza San Marco setting, bargains are few and far between.

➕ G12 ✉ Procuratie Vecchie, Piazza San Marco 125 ☎ 041 522 4464 🚤 Vallaresso 1, 82

MISSONI

Another of the big Italian fashion names, best known for highly colored knitwear and similarly innovative linens and casualwear.

➕ G12–G13 ✉ Calle Vallaresso, San Marco 1312 ☎ 041 520 5733 🚤 Vallaresso 1, 82

MONDO NOVO

The masks in this attractive store just south of Campo Santa Margherita are definitely superior to the mediocre versions in lesser stores around the city. A wonderful place for children and adults alike.

➕ D12 ✉ Rio Terrà Canal, Dorsoduro 3063 ☎ 041 528 7344 🚤 Ca' Rezzonico 1

NARDI

Rivals Missiaglia (see opposite) for the title of Venice's smartest jeweler. High prices.

➕ G12 ✉ Procuratie Nuove, Piazza San Marco 69 ☎ 041 522 5733 🚤 Vallaresso 1, 82

TROIS

This beautiful old shop is the only place in Venice where you can still buy original Fortuny fabrics—choose from stunning lengths down to cushion covers and browse among the beadwork, though all this elegance comes at a price.

➕ F13 ✉ Campo San Maurizio, San Marco 2666 ☎ 041 522 2905 🚤 Vallaresso 1, 82

VALENTINO

The doyen of Rome *alta moda* and stylish ready-to-wear clothes has a store just west of Piazza San Marco, close to the stores of other leading names in the world of fashion.

➕ G12 ✉ Salizzada San Moisè, San Marco 1473 ☎ 041 520 5733 🚤 Vallaresso 1, 82

VENEZIARTIGIANA

A perfect place to shop for gifts, this store collects the work of numerous local craftspeople under one roof: choose from masks, silverware, jewelry, ceramics, wood creations, pictures, posters, and a host of other beautiful objects.

➕ F13–G12 ✉ Calle Larga (Viale) XXII Marzo, San Marco 412–13 🚤 Vallaresso or Santa Maria del Giglio 1, 82

MARIANO FORTUNY

Fortuny was born in Catalonia, Spain in 1871, the son of a painter and fabric collector. He moved to Venice when he was 18, soon gaining renown in fields ranging from physics and chemistry to architecture and theater design. Today, he is best remembered for his fabrics, and in particular for the pleated dresses he created that were so fine they could be rolled up and threaded through a wedding ring.

Books, Paper & Stationery

ANTIQUES

Bric-a-brac and antique bargains are rare in a city that is acutely aware of its past and the value of its objets d'art. Still, Venice provides an almost unlimited choice of beautiful things to buy. Antique stores are dotted around the city; the largest concentrations are around San Maurizio and Santa Maria Zobenigo just east of Campo Santo Stefano (Campo Francesco Morosini ✚ F12–F13). Slightly less expensive stores can be found in the area around San Barnaba (✚ D12). The most famous stores are Paolo Scarpa's two outlets at Campo San Moisè, San Marco 1464 (✚ G12), and Calle Larga (Viale) XXII Marzo, San Marco 2089 (✚ F13–G12). Regular flea and antique markets are held in Campo San Maurizio; contact the tourist office for dates.

EBRÛ

The owner of this store, Alberto Valese, was at the cutting edge of the 1970s revival in Venetian marbled paper. His store takes its name from the traditional Turkish marbling technique used to create many of his products. Some of the smaller items make ideal gifts or souvenirs to take home.
✚ F12 ✉ Campo Santo Stefano, San Marco 3471 ☎ 041 523 8830 🚤 Santa Maria del Giglio 1

FANTONI

This well-known store contains the city's largest selection of big, glossy art books.
✚ F12–G12 ✉ Salizzada San Luca, San Marco 4119 ☎ 041 522 0700 🚤 Rialto 1, 82

FILIPPI EDITORE VENEZIA

This specialist store is renowned for its large collection of books on all aspects of Venice (mostly in Italian) and its many facsimile editions of old books.
✚ G11 ✉ Calle della Casselleria, San Marco 5284 ☎ 041 523 6916 🚤 Rialto 1, 82

GOLDONI

Well stocked and by common consent the best general bookstore in the city, Goldini has a wide range of literature on the city, along with a limited selection of English and other foreign-language titles.
✚ G12 ✉ Calle dei Fabbri,
San Marco 4742 ☎ 041 522 2384 🚤 Vallaresso 1, 82

IL PAPIRO

A fine little store selling marbled paper and other pretty stationery. There is another outlet in Castello.
✚ F12 ✉ Calle del Piovan, San Marco 2764 ☎ 041 522 3055 (both shops) 🚤 Santa Maria del Giglio 1

LEGATORIA PIAZZESI

Established in 1900, this is one of the last workshops in the city to use traditional wood-block methods to hand-print its beautiful papers, books, and stationery. Expensive.
✚ F12 ✉ Campiello della Feltrina, San Marco 2511 ☎ 041 522 1202 🚤 Santa Maria del Giglio 1

PAOLO OLBI

Another artisan at the forefront of the revival of marbled paper. Olbi's appealing store sells a wide range of marbled stationery and ornaments that make the perfect gift.
✚ F12 ✉ Calle della Mandola, San Marco 3653 ☎ 041 528 5025 🚤 Sant'Angelo 1

POLLIERO

A tiny, old-fashioned store alongside Santa Maria Gloriosa dei Frari, Polliero sells a lovely selection of leather-bound and marbled paper stationery, together with handmade gifts and beautiful individual sheets of paper.
✚ E11 ✉ Campo dei Frari, San Polo 2995 ☎ 041 528 5130 🚤 San Tomà 1, 82

Food & Drink

ALIANI (CASA DEL PARMIGIANO)

Perhaps Venice's most famous delicatessen, this store has a superlative selection of cheeses, together with a variety of hams, salamis, fresh pasta, and other ready-made delicacies.

➕ F11 ✉ Campo della Corderia, Ruga Vecchia San Giovanni, San Polo 214 ☎ 041 520 6525 🚤 Rialto or San Silvestro 1, 82

ERBERIA

Venice's main outdoor market provides a wonderful spectacle of sound and color, its stalls laden with fruit and vegetables, its thoroughfares busy with shoppers and traders. Explore the maze of stalls north of Campo San Giacomo di Rialto, not merely the more touristy stalls that line the Ruga degli Orefici.

➕ G11 ✉ Campo San Giacomo di Rialto ⏰ Mon–Sat 7–1 🚤 Rialto 1, 82

MARKETS

Market stalls are in the following locations: Campo Santa Margherita (➕ D12); Campo Santa Maria Formosa (➕ H11); Campiello dell'Anconetta-Rio Terrà San Leonardo (➕ E9); the boats moored on Rio della Tana (➕ K13–L13); and, most evocatively, the famous covered barge by the Ponte dei Pugni on Fondamenta Gerardini (➕ D12).

MASCARI

A specialty food store near the Rialto known for its teas, coffees, seeds, and dried goods.

➕ F11 ✉ Ruga dei Spezieri, San Polo 380 ☎ 041 522 9762 🚤 Rialto or San Silvestro 1, 82

PASTICCERIA MARCHINI

Delicious cakes, cookies, pastries, and sweetmeats from Venice's finest *pasticceria*.

➕ F13 ✉ Ponte San Maurizio, San Marco 2769 ☎ 041 522 9109 🚤 Santa Maria del Giglio 1

PESCHERIA

Venice's evocative fish market, its stalls loaded with all manner of exotic-looking fish and seafood, merges seamlessly with the fruit and vegetable stalls of the adjoining Erberia (see opposite).

➕ F11–G11 ✉ Campo della Pescaria ⏰ Tue–Sat 7–1 🚤 Rialto 1, 82

WINE

Old-fashioned wine store, where you can take empty bottles to be filled from wooden barrels or wicker-wrapped vats, still dot most Venetian neighborhoods. The wine—which can also be bought in bottles—is good and inexpensive, and embraces most of the Veneto's many varieties, including some that are hard to find elsewhere. Wine bars also sell wine by the bottle to take away (► 78). The following La Nave d'Oro outlets are typical:

➕ D12 ✉ Campo Santa Margherita, Dorsoduro 3664; ➕ H11 ✉ Calle del Mondo Novo, Castello 5786; ➕ E9 ✉ Rio Terrà San Leonardo, Cannaregio 1370

PRACTICALITIES

Food stores and bakeries are usually open 8:30–1 and 4–7, though virtually all close on Wednesday afternoons and Sundays. Food served by weight (including bread) is sold by the *chilo, mezzo chilo* (kilo and half-kilo: about 2lb and 1lb) and, more commonly, by the *etto* (100g: about 4oz), plural *etti*.

THE RIALTO

As a district the Rialto is almost as old as the city itself, the earliest settlers having been attracted to its high banks, or *rivo alto*, these forming a dry and easily defended redoubt amidst the marsh and mud of the lagoon. While San Marco developed into the city's political heart, the Rivoaltus became its commercial center, where all manner of staple and exotic goods were traded in the "Bazaar of Europe." The first private banks appeared here in 1157, these soon followed (in 1161) by the Banco di Piazza, Europe's state bank. It did not take long for the tax collectors, magistrates, and other offices of state to appear in their wake.

After Dark

WHAT'S ON

Details of movies, concerts, and exhibitions in Venice are listed in the *"Spettacoli"* section of daily editions of local newspapers such as *Il Gazzettino* and *La Nuova Venezia*. *Un Ospite di Venezia*, a free Italian/English magazine available from hotels and tourist offices, also contains detailed listings (published weekly in peak season, monthly during off-season). Tourist offices always have plenty of posters and leaflets on current events. Also keep an eye open for posters on the streets.

CASINÒ

Venice's popular Casinò Municipale (Municipal Casino), one of only a handful in Italy, is housed in winter in the Palazzo Vendramin-Calergi, one of the Grand Canal's most impressive palaces. From mid-June until mid-September it moves to the Lido at the Palazzo del Casinò. Dress smartly, and take along your passport. ✚ F9–F10 ⊠ Palazzo Vendramin-Calergi, Calle Larga Vendramin, off Rio Terrà della Maddalena, Cannaregio ☎ 041 710211 🕐 Mid-Sep–mid-Jun: daily 8:15PM–2:30AM 🚤 San Marcuola 1, 82 🅿 Dress code smart; ✚ J17–K17 ⊠ Palazzo del Casinò, Piazzale del Casinò, Lungomare G Marconi, Lido ☎ 041 529 7111 🕐 Mid-Jun–mid-Sep: daily 8:15PM–2:30AM 🚤 Casinò or Santa Maria Elisabetta 1, 6, 40, 41, 52, 82 🅿 Dress code smart

MOVIES

Considering the fact that Venice hosts one of Europe's leading movie festivals, it seems astonishing that it has just six movie theaters. Art-house, classic, or original-language movies are screened occasionally at the so-called Cinema d'Essai, but virtually all foreign and current-release movies are dubbed into Italian. The city's principal movie theaters are listed below.
Accademia ✚ E13 ⊠ Calle Corfù, Dorsoduro 1018 ☎ 041 528 7706 🚤 Accademia 1, 3, 4, 82; **Centrale** ✚ G12 ⊠ Piscina da Frezzeria, San Marco 1659 ☎ 041 522 8201 🚤 Vallaresso 1, 3, 4, 82; **Ritz** ✚ G12 ⊠ Calle dei

Segretaria, near Campo San Zulian, San Marco 617 ☎ 041 520 4429 🚤 Vallaresso 1, 3, 4, 82; **Rossini** ✚ E12 ⊠ Calle delle Muneghe, San Marco 4000 ☎ 041 523 0322 🚤 San Samuele 3, 4, 82

CLASSICAL MUSIC

Venice's main classical music spot is La Fenice (see "Opera" ➤ 85), a lovely building which, until it was gutted by fire, presented a winter opera season and a summer season of miscellaneous classical concerts. In its (temporary) absence the city's main classical music venue is La Pietà, Vivaldi's former church, which presents regular concerts of the Venetian composer's work plus other occasional recitals. Tickets are rather expensive, and often pricier than the performance merits. Concerts are also held in the churches of San Stae, Santo Stefano, Santa Maria Gloriosa dei Frari, San Barnaba, and the Ospedaletto, and at the Palazzo Prigione Vecchie, the Palasport dell'Arsenale, and the Scuola Grande di San Giovanni Evangelista. Keep your eyes open for posters advertising concerts, or inquire at the tourist office regarding forthcoming events (➤ 89). The state radio network, RAI, allows the public into recordings of its concerts in the Palazzo Labia, though the free tickets must be reserved in advance (see below). Several small foundations also organize occasional recitals, most notably the

Cini Foundation, based at San Giorgio Maggiore, and the Ugo and Olga Levi Foundation, based at the Palazzo Giustinian-Lolin (inquire at the tourist office for details). The Amici della Musica is a "club" next to the Miracoli church which holds small concerts, art exhibitions, and nightly readings of prose and poetry.

Amici della Musica 🞧 G11 ✉ Campo Miracoli ☎ 041 523 0616 🚊 Rialto 1, 3, 82; **La Pietà** (Santa Maria della Pietà o della Visitazione) 🞧 H12 ✉ Riva degli Schiavoni ☎ 041 523 1096 🚊 San Zaccaria 1, 52, 82 🎫 Tickets expensive; **RAI** 🞧 E9 ✉ Palazzo Labia, Campo San Geremia ☎ 041 524 2812 🚊 Ferrovia 1, 52, 82

CLUBS

Venice has a reputation as a rather sleepy place, and young Venetians often complain about its lack of nightlife. The majority of the region's big discos and clubs are in Mestre and distant Jesolo on the mainland (see newspaper listings for details), while the closest any big bands get to the city for concerts is Padua or Verona. Venice's only "disco" is the rather unhip Il Piccolo Mondo, a bar from 10AM to 8PM, and disco from 8PM to around 4AM. Livelier, more fashionable and more popular among the young is the atmospheric Paradiso Perduto, a bar-restaurant with occasional live music. Harry's Dolci, on the Giudecca, is a smart café-restaurant that has occasional jazz concerts.

Also try Casanova, which combines a restaurant selling light meals with dancing and an internet café.

Harry's Dolci 🞧 D14 ✉ Fondamenta San Biagio, Giudecca 773 ☎ 041 522 4844 🕐 Apr–Oct: daily 10:30AM–3PM, 7:30–10:30PM. Nov–Mar: closed Tue 🚊 Sant'Eufemia 41, 42; **Il Piccolo Mondo** 🞧 E13 ✉ Calle Contarini Corfù, Dorsoduro 1056/a ☎ 041 520 0371 🕐 Bar 10AM–8PM. Disco 10PM–4AM 🚊 Accademia 1, 82; **Paradiso Perduto** 🞧 F9 ✉ Fondamenta della Misericordia, Cannaregio 2540 ☎ 041 720581 🕐 Closed Wed 🚊 San Marcuola or Madonna dell' Orto 1, 52, 82; **Casanova** 🞧 D10 ✉ Lista di Spagna, Cannaregio 145 ☎ 041 275 0199 🚊 Ferrovia 1, 82

OPERA

The catastrophic fire at La Fenice ("The Phoenix") on January 29, 1996 has put Venice's famous opera house out of action for the foreseeable future. Plans to rebuild and restore its once magnificent interior are well advanced, though it is almost impossible to know when the hall will finally reopen for performances. In the meantime, temporary venues have been arranged for opera performances. The main location is the Palafenice on the Isola Nuova del Tronchetto.

Teatro La Fenice 🞧 F12 ✉ Campo San Fantin, San Marco ☎ 041 521 0161 🚊 Santa Maria del Giglio 1 **PalaFenice** 🞧 A9 ✉ Isola Nuova del Tronchetto ☎ 041 520 4010 🚊 Tronchetto 3, 4, 82

EVENING PASTIMES

Venice does not have the nightlife to match other major cities. For many Venetians an evening out consists of a meal or drink with friends rounded off with a stroll to a bar for a coffee or ice cream. One of the best places to join them is Campo Santa Margherita, a square full of easy-going bars and cafés in the student district of Dorsoduro (🞧 D12). Other similar squares include Campo San Polo (🞧 E11–F11), Campo Santo Stefano (Campo Francesco Morosini 🞧 F12), Campo San Barnaba (🞧 D12), and Campo Santa Maria Formosa (🞧 H11). Indeed, few cities can compare with Venice when it comes to atmospheric evening strolls. Certainly none can provide the experience of a gondola or *vaporetto* ride on the Grand Canal.

Festivals

REGATA STORICA

The Regata Storica ("Historic Regatta"; first Sunday in September) is the most famous of several annual regattas held in and around the city each year. A huge flotilla of beautifully decorated craft, their crews in period dress, travels in colorful procession down the Grand Canal (note that onlookers are expected to dress the part too). Races are then held, the most exciting being those between rival gondoliers.

MARRIAGE TO THE SEA

This ceremony began around AD 1000, when Doge Pietro Orseolo II set sail to attack Dalmatia, among the first of Venice's conquests. Originally a libation before battle, in time it came to symbolize the Republic's naval power and special relationship with the sea. The doge and his retinue would sail into the lagoon, there dropping a golden ring into the water and reciting the words: "We espouse thee, O sea, in sign of our real and perpetual dominion over thee." Divers then competed to find the ring, the winner–if any–earning relief from "all the burdens to which dwellers in the Republic are subject." These days a laurel wreath is used instead of a golden ring.

CARNEVALE

Venice's famous carnival takes its name from the Latin *carnem levare*, or *carne vale*—the "farewell to meat." It probably began in the city's 15th-century private clubs, whose members indicated their allegiances by wearing different colored hose. Although the clubs initially limited themselves to boat races and social frivolities, they eventually took to competing in masked balls on Martedì Grasso, the prelude to Lent. Resurrected in 1979 (by a group of non-Venetians), it emulates the great pre-Lenten festivals of the 18th century, thousands of tourists dressing in masks and extravagant costumes to indulge in a series of enthusiastically supported events. Today, the carnival officially lasts just ten days (up to the beginning of Lent), though the event has become so large—and so commercialized—that Venice often has to close the causeway to cars for the duration.

FESTA DEL REDENTORE

The Festa del Redentore is the more spectacular of the two major festivals held to celebrate Venice's deliverance from past epidemics (the other is the Festa della Salute; see below). Observed on the third Sunday of July, it commemorates the end of the 1576 plague, an epidemic that wiped out a third of the city's inhabitants. In times past the doge and his entourage would visit the church of the Redentore, crossing to the Giudecca on a pontoon of boats thrown across the Canale della Giudecca. Today, Venetians stream across a similar bridge on the Saturday evening, many taking to boats for a traditional picnic on the water.

FESTA DELLA SALUTE

Like the Festa del Redentore, the feast of La Salute (November 21) commemorates Venice's deliverance from bubonic plague, in this case the epidemic of 1630 which again claimed an estimated one-third of the city's population. Ever since, Venetians have crossed a pontoon bridge thrown across the Grand Canal to Santa Maria della Salute (built to mark the end of the plague; ➤ 36), to give thanks for their health (*salute*) and to pray for sick friends and relations.

LA SENSA

The feast of the La Sensa (Sunday after Ascension Day) is a resurrected version of the ancient Marriage to the Sea ceremony (see panel). The city mayor, his or her retinue and assorted VIPs sail out onto the lagoon on a copy of the *Bucintoro*, the old dogal state barge. Also in May is the more impressive Vogalonga, or "Long Row," during which boats compete in a 20-mile race to the island of Burano and back.

VENICE
travel facts

ESSENTIAL FACTS

Electricity

- Current is 220 volts AC (50 cycles), but is suitable for 240-volt appliances.
- Plugs are of the Continental two-round-pin variety.

Etiquette

- Do not wear shorts or miniskirts and cover your arms in churches.
- Do not intrude while church services are in progress.
- Do not eat or drink in churches.
- Many churches and galleries forbid flash photography, or ban photography altogether.
- There are few no-smoking areas in restaurants or public places, but smoking is banned on all public transportation (including boats).

Money

- Foreign-exchange facilities are available at banks and kiosks throughout the city.
- Major credit cards are widely accepted in Venice and can be used in ATMs displaying the appropriate sign.

National holidays

- Jan 1: New Year's Day
- Jan 6: Epiphany
- Easter Sunday
- Easter Monday
- Apr 25: Liberation Day
- May 1: Labor Day
- Aug 15: Assumption
- Nov 1: All Saints' Day
- Dec 8: Immaculate Conception
- Dec 25: Christmas Day
- Dec 26: Santo Stefano
- Nov 21: Stores and businesses may also close or observe shorter hours during the Festa della Salute
- Good Friday is not a holiday

Opening hours

- Banks: Mon–Fri 8–1:30 (larger branches also 3–4).
- Churches: No fixed hours, but generally Mon–Sat 9–noon, 3–6; Sun 2–5; except Basilica di San Marco: 9:45–5 (10–4 in winter).
- Museums: Varied, but state-run galleries generally Tue–Sat 9–2, Sun 9–1; city-run and private museums such as the Correr, Palazzo Ducale and Guggenheim usually open all day.
- Post offices: Mon–Sat 8–1:30, though small offices may not open on Sat, while main offices remain open 8–7 for some services.
- Restaurants: Many close on Sun evening and all day Mon, plus a statutory closing day once a week (*la chiusura settimanale*).
- Stores: Generally 9–1, 4–8; most food stores close Wed afternoons except in summer, while other stores close Mon mornings except in summer.

Places of worship

- Anglican: St. George's ✚ E13 ✉ Campo San Vio, Dorsoduro 871 ☎ 041 520 0571
- Catholic (English mass): San Moisè ✚ G12 ✉ Campo San Moisè, San Marco; Basilica di San Marco ✚ G–H12 ✉ Piazza San Marco; Gesuiti ✚ G–H10 ✉ Campo dei Gesuiti; Scalzi ✚ D10 ✉ Fondamenta degli Scalzi; Santi Giovanni e Paolo ✚ H11 ✉ Campo Santi Giovanni e Paolo; The Redentore ✚ F15 ✉ Campo Redentore, Giudecca; San Giorgio Maggiore ✚ H14 ✉ Isola di San Giorgio Maggiore
- Jewish: ✚ E9 ✉ Ghetto Vecchio ☎ 041 715012

Restrooms

- Restrooms are at Piazzale Roma ✚ C11; the train station ✚ C10–D10; the west side of the Accademia bridge ✚ E13; off Campo San Bartolomeo ✚ G11; by the Giardinetti Reali ✚ G12–G13; on Calle Erizzo near the church of San Martino ✚ J12; and in the Albergo Diurno (Day Hotel) behind the Ala Napoleonica on Ramo Primo a Ascensione ✚ G12

- In bars and cafés ask for *il gabinetto* or *il bagno*.
- Do not confuse *signori* (men) with *signore* (women).

Tourist information

- Main tourist offices ✚ G13 ✉ Venice Pavilion, Palazzina del Santi by the Giardinetti Reali ☎ 041 522 5150; ✚ G12 ✉ Piazza San Marco 71/c (Ascensione) ☎ 041 529 8730; fax 041 528 8730 ⏱ Summer: Mon–Sat 9:10–6:50. Winter: Mon–Sat 9:30–3:30
- Train station office ✚ D10 ☎ 041 241 1499 or 041 529 8711; hotel booking agency 041 715016 or 041 715288 ⏱ Daily 8AM–7/9PM
- Marco Polo Airport office ☎ 041 541 5887 ⏱ Summer: 9–1, 2–6. Winter: 9:30–3:30
- Lido office ✚ L16 ✉ Gran Viale Santa Maria Elisabetta 6 ☎ 041 526 5721 ⏱ Summer: 8:30–7:30. Winter: 9:30–3:30

PUBLIC TRANSPORTATION

Boats

- ACTV runs two basic types of boat: the general-purpose *vaporetto*, and the faster *motoscafo*. Both follow set routes and are numbered at the front of the boat. As the same number boat may run in two directions (up and down the Grand Canal, for example), it is vital at the quays—which usually have separate boarding points for each direction—to make sure you board a boat heading in the right direction. This is particularly true at the Ferrovia and San Zaccaria, both busy termini for several routes.

- The web of boat routes around Venice is not as confusing as it first seems. The basic route is Line 1 along the Grand Canal (Piazzale Roma–Vallaresso–Lido and back). Line 82 also follows the Grand Canal, but has fewer stops. A second 82 boat runs from San Zaccaria to Piazzale Roma by way of the Giudecca. The other boat you may use is Line 12, which runs to the islands of Murano, Burano, and Torcello from the Fondamente Nuove. The ferry information throughout this guide gives the nearest stop as well as the line number.

- Tickets can be bought at most landing stages, on board boats (with a surcharge), and at stores or tobacconists with an ACTV sticker. One-way and return flat-fare tickets are valid along the length of the route so the price is the same for one stop or ten stops. Tickets must be validated in machines at each landing stage before boarding. Spot fines are levied if you are caught traveling without a ticket.

- Four tourist tickets are available (►7)

- ACTV runs a less frequent service with a reduced number of stops throughout the night on key Grand Canal routes. Exact times are posted on the timetables at every quay. Tickets can be bought on board.

Water taxis

- Venice's water taxis are fast but extremely expensive. The basic rate is around 18 euros; L35,000 for seven minutes, plus 0.25 euros; L500 for every additional 15 seconds. Surcharges are levied for each piece of luggage, for trips between 10PM and 7AM, and for each additional passenger over a maximum of four. You can hail a taxi on a canal, but it is usually easier to call by phone—which means around 5 euros; L10,000 on the clock before you start ☎ 041 523 5775, 041 522 2303, 041 716124, 041 522 1265, or 041 523 0575; airport 041 541 5084

Taxis

- For rides to and from the mainland there are taxi stands at Piazzale Roma ☎ 041 523 2473; Marco Polo Airport ☎ 041 526 5975; and at the railroad station at Mestre ☎ 041 522 8538. Otherwise, call Radio Taxi ☎ 041 936222

Traghetti

- As there are only three bridges across the Grand Canal, Venice's *traghetti* (ferries) provide an invaluable service. Using old gondolas, they ply back and forth at seven strategic points. Quays are usually obscure, so look for the little yellow "Traghetto" signs. Crossings cost around 0.5 euros; L800, which you hand to the ferryman as you board. Venetians usually stand, but nobody minds if you sit unless the boat is crowded. Be careful with small children, and watch your balance when the boat pushes off.

For further information on public transportation ➤ 7.

MEDIA & COMMUNICATIONS

Newspapers & magazines

- Venice's two main local newspapers are *Il Gazzettino* and *La Nuova Venezia*. Both contain listings for the city.
- Quality national papers include the center-left *La Repubblica* and center-right *Corriere della Sera*.
- *Corriere dello Sport* and the *Gazzetta dello Sport*, two exclusively sports-based papers, are also popular.
- News magazines (*riviste*) such as *L'Espresso* and *Panorama* also enjoy a large readership.
- Foreign newspapers are readily available in Venice, usually from late afternoon on the day of issue. Kiosks at the train station are the best source.

Radio & television

- Italian radio and television have many deregulated national and local stations, including several based in the Veneto region around Venice. Major national television stations divide between the channels of the state RAI network (RAI 1, 2, and 3) and the channels founded by Silvio Berlusconi (Canale 5, Rete 4, and Italia Uno).

Post offices

- Venice's central post office (*posta* or *ufficio postale*) is near the Rialto bridge ✚ G11 ✉ Palazzo delle Poste, Fondaco dei Tedeschi ☎ 041 271 7111 🕐 Mon–Sat 8–7; foreign exchange (upstairs) 8–6
- Another office lies just west of Piazza San Marco ✚ G12 ✉ Calle dell'Ascensione ☎ 041 528 5949 🕐 Mon–Fri 8:10–1:30; Sat 8:10–12:30
- Stamps (*francobolli*) are available from post offices, or from tobacco stores (*tabacchi*) displaying a blue "T" sign.
- Mailboxes are small and red and are marked *Poste* or *Lettere*. They usually have two slots—one for local mail (*Città*), the other for destinations further afield (*Altre Destinazione*).
- International mail sent to and from Venice can take up to three weeks to arrive. You can speed things up

by sending post *espresso* (express) or *raccomandata* (registered).

- Address poste restante letters Fermo Posta, Fondaco dei Tedeschi, 30100 Venezia. Mail can be collected Mon–Sat 8:15AM–7PM. Take a passport when collecting mail and be prepared to pay a small fee. Filing can be haphazard, so ask staff to check under both your first and last names.

Telephones

- Telecom Italia (TI) provides public telephones in bars, on the streets and in TI offices. All are indicated by red or yellow signs showing a telephone dial and receiver. Venice has TI booths in Piazzale Roma ✚ C11 🕐 8AM–9:30PM; and the main post office; ✚ G11 ✉ Fondaco dei Tedeschi 🕐 8:15–7
- Public phones accept coins and phone cards (*schede telefoniche*), available from tobacco stores, TI offices, automatic dispensers, or stores displaying a TI sticker. Remember to tear the corner off the card before using it.
- Peak periods are weekdays 8–1, off-peak is 1–8, and calls are cheap at all other times. The cheap international rate covers the weekend and 8PM–8AM during the week.
- The dial tone is alternating long and short pips. A series of rapid pips means you are being connected, while a series of long beeps indicates a ringing telephone at the other end. More rapid beeps means "engaged."
- For international calls, use a phone card or a *telefono a scatti*—a kiosk where you speak first and pay when your call is over (in some bars, hotels, post offices, and tourist offices, and in most TI offices). Dial 011 for an inter-

national line followed by the country code. The code for Italy when calling from abroad is 39.

- To make a collect call, dial 15 (Europe) or 170 (intercontinental) and ask to make *una chiamata con pagamento a destinazione*.
- The area code for Venice is 041 and must be used when calling from outside and within Venice (numbers in this book include the code).

EMERGENCIES

Consulates
- Australia ✉ Via Borgogna 22, Milan ☎ 02 777041
- Austria ✉ Santa Croce 251 ☎ 041 524 0556
- Belgium ✉ San Marco 1470 ☎ 041 522 4124
- Canada ✉ Riviera Ruzzante 25, Padua ☎ 049 878 147
- Denmark ✉ San Marco 466/g ☎ 041 520 0822
- France ✉ Zattere 1397 ☎ 041 522 4319
- Netherlands ✉ San Marco 2888 ☎ 041 528 3416
- Norway ✉ Santa Croce 466/b ☎ 041 523 1345
- Republic of Ireland ✉ Piazza Campitelli 3, Rome ☎ 06 697 9121
- Switzerland ✉ Zattere, Dorsoduro 810 ☎ 041 522 5996
- U.K. ✉ Dorsoduro 1051 ☎ 041 522 7207
- U.S.A. ✉ Via Principe Amedeo 2/10, Milan ☎ 02 290351

Emergency phone numbers
- Emergency services (police, fire, and ambulance) ☎ 113
- Police (*Carabinieri*) ☎ 112
- Questura (Venice Police Station) ☎ 041 271 5511
- Fire (*Vigili di Fuoco*) ☎ 115/113
- Ambulance ☎ 041 523 0000 or 113
- Hospital and first aid (Ospedale Civile) ☎ 041 529 4517

Health

- Likely hazards include too much sun, air pollution, and biting insects.
- Water is safe to drink unless marked *acqua non potabile*.
- Pharmacies (*una farmacia*) are identified by a green cross and have the same opening hours as stores, but open late on some days as displayed on pharmacy doors. Staff can give advice on minor ailments and dispense many medicines over the counter, including some only available on prescription in other countries. Remember to bring any prescriptions that might be required to obtain medicine.
- If you wish to see a doctor (*un medico*), inquire at your hotel. For first aid (*pronto soccorso*) or hospital treatment, visit the Ospedale Civile ✚ H10–H11 ✉ Campo Santi Giovanni e Paolo, Castello ☎ 041 529 4517
- Vaccinations are unnecessary for entry into Italy unless you are traveling from a known infected area. Check current requirements if you are traveling from the Far East, Africa, South America, or the Middle East.

Lost property

- City streets ☎ 041 520 8844
- Buses or boats ☎ 041 528 7886 (Mon–Sat 8–6/4:30 in winter)
- Train or station ☎ 041 785238
- Airport ☎ 041 260 6436
- Report losses of passports to the police and your consulate.
- Report general losses to the main police station ✉ Questura, Via San Nicolodi 22, Marghera ☎ 041 271 5511

Sensible precautions

- Venice's many tourists are an obvious target for the unscrupulous, but by using common sense and taking a few precautions you should stay safe. Report thefts to your hotel and then to the main police station, which has a department to deal with your problems ✉ Questura, Via San Nicolodi 22, Marghera ☎ 041 271 5511. They will issue you with a document (*una denuncia*) to send in with your insurance claims. Report lost passports to the police and your consulate or embassy.
- Carry cash in a belt or pouch, never in a pocket.
- Do not carry large amounts of cash. Use credit cards or traveler's checks.
- Wear your camera and never put it down on café tables. Beware of strap-cutting thieves.
- Do not flaunt valuables. Leave jewelry in the hotel safe (if it has one), especially items such as chains and earrings that can easily be snatched.
- Hold bags across your front, not just hung over one shoulder where they can be rifled or grabbed.
- Beware of pickpockets on water buses, in markets, or wherever groups of tourists gather.
- After dark, avoid noncommercial parts of the city, parks, and the area around the train station.
- Always lock your car, and never leave luggage or valuables inside.
- Women visiting Venice on their own should have few problems in the city, which is generally extremely safe.

LANGUAGE

- Italians respond well to foreigners who make an effort to speak their language, however badly. Many speak at least some English, and most upscale hotels and restaurants have multilingual staff.

- All Italian words are pronounced as written, with each vowel and consonant sounded. The letter *c* is hard, as in English "cat," except when followed by *i* or *e*, when it becomes the soft ch of "children." The same applies to *g* when followed by *i* or *e*—soft in *giardino*, as in the English "giant"; hard in *gatto*, as in "gate." Words ending in *o* are almost always masculine in gender (plural ending—*i*); those ending in *a* are feminine (plural ending—*e*).
- Use the polite third person (*lei*) to speak to strangers and the second person (*tu*) to friends or children.

Courtesies

good morning buon giorno
good afternoon/good evening buona sera
good night buona notte
hello/goodbye (informal) ciao
hello (answering the telephone) pronto
goodbye arrivederci
please per favore
thank you (very much) (mille) grazie
you're welcome prego
how are you? (polite/informal) come sta/stai?
I'm fine sto bene
I'm sorry mi dispiace
excuse me/I beg your pardon (formal) mi scusi
excuse me (in a crowd) permesso

Basic vocabulary

yes sì
no no
I do not understand non ho capito
left/right sinistra/destra
entrance entrata
exit uscita
open/closed aperto/chiuso
upstairs sopra
downstairs da basso

come in! avanti!
good/bad buono/cattivo
big/small grande/piccolo
with con
without senza
more più
less meno
near vicino
far lontano
hot/cold caldo/freddo
early presto
late ritardo
now adesso
later più tardi
today oggi
tomorrow domani
yesterday ieri
morning mattino
afternoon pomeriggio
how much is it? quant'è?
expensive caro
inexpensive a buon mercato
when? quando?
do you have ...? avete ...?

Emergencies

help! aiuto!
where is the nearest telephone? dov'è il telefono più vicino?
there has been an accident c'è stato un incidente
call the police chiamate la polizia
call a doctor/an ambulance chiamate un medico/un'ambulanza
first aid pronto soccorso
where is the nearest hospital? dov'è l'ospedale più vicino?

Numbers

one uno, una
two due
three tre
four quattro
five cinque
six sei
seven sette
eight otto
nine nove
ten dieci

Index

Citypack
Venice

AUTHOR AND EDITION REVISER *Tim Jepson*
COVER DESIGN *Tigist Getachew, Fabrizio La Rocca*
MANAGING EDITOR *Jackie Staddon*

ISBN 0–676–90173–5

THIRD EDITION

ACKNOWLEDGMENTS

The Automobile Association wishes to thank the following photographers and libraries for their assistance in the preparation of this book:
AKG LONDON 161, 171 (Cameraphoto); ARCAID 8/9 (Joe Cornish); BRIDGEMAN ART LIBRARY 16r Procession in St. Mark's Square, detail of the Basilica, 1496 (oil on canvas) by Gentile Bellini (c1419–1507) Galleria dell'Accademia, Venice, 33 Supper at the house of Levi, 1573 by Veronese, (Paolo Caliari), Galleria dell'Accademia, Venice, 52 The Miracle of the Cross on San Lorenzo Bridge, 1500 by Gentile Bellini, Galleria dell'Accademia, Venice, 53b St. George Killing the Dragon by Carpaccio, Vittore, Scuola di San Giorgio degli Schiavoni, Venice; ROBERT HARDING PICTURE LIBRARY 8bl, 11cb, 12/3, 13r, 14c, 21l; JOHN HESELTINE ARCHIVE 44; PICTOR INTERNATIONAL, LONDON 14/5, 241; SPECTRUM COLOUR LIBRARY 26b; STOCKBYTE 5; TOPHAM PICTUREPOINT 17r. The remaining pictures are held in the Association's own library (AA PHOTO LIBRARY) with contributions from: SIMON MCBRIDE 1t, 1b, 2t, 4t, 6t, 7tr, 8tl, 9tr, 10t, 10/1t, 10/1b, 10tl, 11ct, 12t, 12l, 13tl, 13l, 14t, 14l, 15tl, 16t, 18, 18t, 19r, 20tl, 20l, 22tl, 24t, 24r; DARIO MITIDIERI cover: lion detail, mask, 13tr, 15tr, 19tr, 22tc, 29c, 30, 31t, 32t, 32b, 35t, 37t, 39t, 39b, 41t, 45t, 45b, 47, 48, 51b, 53t, 55, 56, 57b, 59, 60, 61; RICHARD NEWTON cover: gondolier, 25, 34b, 54t; CLIVE SAWYER all cover images with the exception of: lion detail, gondolier, mask, 7tl, 8cl, 9cr, 10tr, 19tl, 20tr, 20r, 21t, 21r, 22tr, 23, 26t, 27, 28, 29t, 31b, 35b, 36t, 36b, 37b, 38, 40t, 40b, 41b, 42t, 42b, 43t, 43b, 46t, 46b, 49b, 50t, 50b, 51t, 54b, 57t, 58, 62, 63t, 63b, 87t, 87b; ROSIE WALFORD 34t, 49t

IMPORTANT NOTE

SPECIAL SALES

Color separation by Daylight Colour Art Pte Ltd, Singapore
Manufactured by Dai Nippon Printing Co. (Hong Kong) Ltd
10 9 8 7 6 5 4 3 2 1

TITLES IN THE CITYPACK SERIES

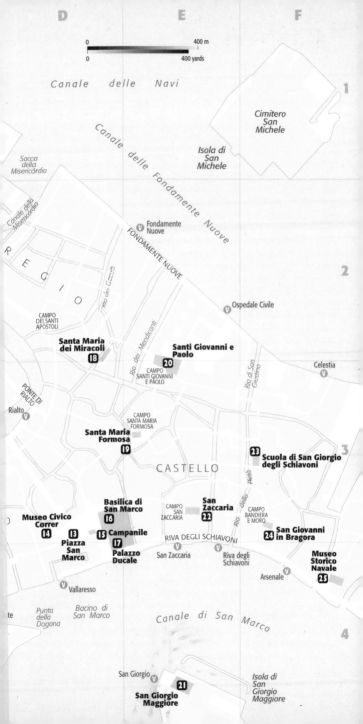

PRAISE FOR FODOR'S CITYPACKS

"Best new city guide we've seen."
–*Southern Living*

"Rich assortment of hotel, restaurant,
and entertainment options. Very attractive."
–*National Geographic Traveler*

"In a word—excellent!"
–*Family Travel Times*

THE CITYPACK MAP COVERS THE CITY IN DETAIL,
WHILE THE CITYPACK GUIDE GIVES YOU JUST
THE INFORMATION YOU NEED TO EXPERIENCE
THE BEST OF VENICE

- Top attractions and their must-see sights

- Great paintings, views and landmarks, churches and squares, children's activities, and freebies

- Offbeat sights even locals don't know

- Tours and excursions

- Restaurants, hotels, shopping, nightlife— with pithy descriptions of each recommendation

- Best festivals and events

- Tips on getting the most from your visit

The author: *Tim Jepson was Rome correspondent for the* Sunday Telegraph *of London and has written and contributed to many books on Italy, where he lived for several years.*

www.fodors.com
links · bookings · traveler-to-traveler advice